BY COMPACT, NOT COMMAND:

Founding-Era Documents on Federalism and Liberty

Introduction, Biographies, and Selection of Documents

by Joe A. Wolverton, II, J.D.

Constitutional Law Scholar, The John Birch Society

Edited by Connor Kimball

WESTERN ISLANDS
PUBLISHING

APPLETON, WISCONSIN

Copyright © June 2025 by Joe Wolverton, II, J.D.
All rights reserved. No portion of this book may be reproduced in any form.

Published by
Western Islands
770 N. Westhill Boulevard
Appleton, Wisconsin 54914
www.JBS.org

Cover Design by Lindsey McConnell

Library of Congress Control Number: 2025936713
International Standard Book Number (ISBN): 978-0-88279-153-1

Printed in the United States of America

Table of Contents

Introduction i

About the Authors iii

A Note from the Editor ix

The Kentucky Resolutions by Thomas Jefferson (1799) 1

The Virginia Resolutions by James Madison (1798) 7

"Report of 1800" by James Madison (1800) 13

A Political Catechism by Maria Pinckney (1830)............ 25

"The Danger Not Over" from the Richmond Examiner, October 1801, by Edmund Pendleton (1801) 43

A Brief Inquiry into the True Nature and Character of Our Federal Government by Abel P. Upshur (1840)........... 51

"The Union" from Constructions Construed and Constitutions Vindicated by John Taylor of Caroline (1820)........... 215

Introduction

In the crucible of revolution and the fervent quest for liberty, the United States emerged as a beacon of democratic governance and as a champion of federalism. The creation of the federal government, as enshrined in the Constitution, was not merely a moment of political innovation – it was a deliberate act of collective sovereignty by the states.

By Compact, Not Command: Founding-Era Documents on Federalism and Liberty is a meticulously curated compilation of writings that illuminates this foundational period. From the simple and sublime truths in *A Political Catechism* to the compelling Kentucky and Virginia Resolutions, these documents offer a plain, persuasive, and passionate defense of the intended relationship between states and the federal government they created. Through these critical texts, the intellectual and philosophical battles that forged the American republic come to life.

By Compact, Not Command is for those who cherish the Constitution and for those who seek to understand the delicate interplay between state and federal powers. It is for learners eager to recover the wisdom of men and women whose influential writings – once commonplace – have been all but erased from the historical record – wisdom which reveals the true nature of constitutional government. More than just an educational resource, this collection serves as a reminder of the enduring principles that shape America's democratic experiment.

However, *By Compact, Not Command* is more than just a historical record. Its writings reaffirm a self-evident truth: the federal government was conceived as an agent of the states, a servant to their collective will, designed to secure the blessings of liberty and prosperity for all. The Constitution itself was formed as a pact among sovereign states, each retaining its sovereignty, freedom, and independence. When properly understood, these principles illuminate the path to restoring constitutional self-government, empowering readers to further safeguard their liberty and the welfare of their country.

Join our Founding Fathers as they unravel the complexities of contemporary government. They challenge us to consider the balance of power, the nature of federalism, and the enduring struggle to preserve liberty and justice for all. Welcome to a journey into the heart of America's constitutional heritage.

About the Authors

Thomas Jefferson (April 13, 1743 – July 4, 1826)

Thomas Jefferson, the third president of the United States and the principal author of the Declaration of Independence, remains one of the most influential figures in American history. Born into a wealthy Virginia family, Jefferson was deeply invested in the Enlightenment ideals – ideals which shaped his views on governance and human rights. His drafting of the Declaration of Independence in 1776 was a seminal moment, articulating not only the colonies' right to secede from the British empire, but also the inherent rights of individuals. The same "self-evident", luminous truths which enshrined the Declaration would later radiate from the Kentucky Resolutions – the right of a people in their state to be the ultimate arbiters of their government shall not be infringed.

As president (1801 – 1809), Jefferson pursued policies that emphasized agrarianism, limited government, and the expansion of the United States – most notably through the Louisiana Purchase in 1803, which doubled the size of the nation. Jefferson's tenure also included efforts to maintain American neutrality amidst European conflicts.

Beyond his political achievements, Jefferson was a voracious scholar, contributing to architecture, archaeology, and education, ultimately founding the University of Virginia as an embodiment of his educational ideals.

Jefferson's writings and ideas, particularly on individual rights and democratic governance, no doubt continue to impress and influence ardent scholars of American civil and political virtues.

James Madison (March 16, 1751 – June 28, 1836)

James Madison, the fourth president of the United States, is celebrated as the principal architect of the U.S. Constitution and as a pivotal figure in the development of the American federal form of government. Born in Port Conway, Virginia, Madison's early interest in governance and philosophy shaped his future contributions to the nation.

His intellectual prowess and vision were instrumental in the drafting of the Constitution during the Philadelphia Convention of 1787, where he advocated for a federal government balanced by checks and balances among its branches. As a co-author of *The Federalist Papers*, alongside Alexander Hamilton and John Jay, Madison vigorously defended the proposed Constitution to a skeptical public. His political philosophy emphasized the importance of limiting governmental power and protecting individual liberties. This was emphasized in the Virginia Resolutions, but no doubt culminating in his drafting of the Bill of Rights.

Madison's presidency (1809 – 1817) was marked by the War of 1812, which, despite initial unpopularity, ultimately solidified the United States' independence from British influence.

Beyond his presidency, Madison's extensive contributions to political theory and his role in the early development of the United States' governmental structure have cemented his legacy as a fundamental figure in American history.

Maria Pinckney (ca. 1776 – May 13, 1836)

Maria Pinckney, a distinguished figure in early American history, was born into a prominent South Carolina family as the eldest daughter of General Charles Cotesworth Pinckney, a notable figure in the Continental Army and a delegate to the 1787 Constitutional Convention, and Sarah "Sally" Middleton. Her lineage included connections to significant figures in the American independence movement, such as her uncle, Arthur Middleton.

Educated and nurtured within a milieu of patriotism and intellectual vigor, Maria's upbringing was marked by a blend of rigorous home education – guided by her grandmother Eliza Lucas Pinckney – and a profound sense of civic duty inherited from her family. This foundation helped shape her into a person of strong character, known for her benevolence, unwavering friendships, and a deep-seated love for her country and state.

Her work emphasized the compact nature of the Federal Constitution, affirming that it was an agreement among sovereign states rather than a creation of a single national body. Pinckney's arguments were rooted in the belief that states did not relinquish their sovereignty upon forming the Constitution. She upheld that the federal government was a creation of the states, bound to serve their collective interests without overriding their individual rights.

Maria Pinckney never married and, after the death of her father's second wife, took on significant familial responsibilities alongside her sister. She passed away on May 13, 1836, and was laid to rest in St. Michael's Churchyard in Charleston, leaving behind a legacy of political thought that would continue to influence discussions of federalism and states' rights.

Edmund Pendleton (September 9, 1721 – October 23, 1803)

Edmund Pendleton was a Virginian statesman, jurist, and patriot who played a pivotal role in the American Revolution and the founding of the Republic. A self-educated lawyer, he rose to prominence as a defender of colonial rights while maintaining a deep respect for order and constitutional government. He served in Virginia's House of Burgesses, the First and Second Continental Congresses, and presided over the state's 1788 ratification convention, where he advocated for the U.S. Constitution.

Despite his Federalist leanings, Pendleton remained wary of centralized power, a concern he expressed in "The Danger Not Over", published in the Richmond *Examiner* in October 1801. In that essay, he warned that the Constitution itself could become a tool of tyranny if its limitations were not strictly enforced. He cautioned against blind trust in government officials, arguing that power, even when granted for noble purposes, has a tendency to expand beyond its rightful bounds. His words resonated with those who feared that the principles of the Revolution were being eroded under the weight of an increasingly assertive federal government.

As president of Virginia's highest court, Pendleton influenced American legal traditions with his commitment to due process and the rule of law. He died on October 23, 1803, leaving behind a legacy of vigilance against tyranny and a reminder that liberty requires eternal defense.

Abel Parker Upshur (June 17, 1790 – February 28, 1844)

Abel Upshur was a prominent figure in early 19th-century American politics, serving as both Secretary of the Navy and Secretary of State under President John Tyler. Born into a planter family in Northampton County, Virginia, Upshur pursued law after attending Yale College and the College of New Jersey (now Princeton University). He was admitted to the Virginia bar in 1810 and started his political career in the Virginia House of Delegates, 1812 to 1813, with a return in 1825 to 1827, before being appointed as a justice to the Virginia General Court in 1826.

Upshur's tenure as Secretary of the Navy (1841 – 1843) was marked by efforts to modernize and expand the Navy, including implementing the bureau system, increasing appropriations, and promoting the construction of new warships. He was a staunch advocate for a strong naval force, aiming for the U.S. Navy to rival the British Royal Navy in size.

In July 1843, Upshur became Secretary of State and championed the annexation of Texas as a state. He was also instrumental in negotiations over the Oregon boundary dispute, which would later contribute to the establishment of the U.S.-Canada border along the 49th parallel. Unfortunately, his tenure was cut short by his tragic death in the USS *Princeton* explosion in 1844.

Upshur's legacy reflects the nation's growing assertiveness on the global stage during the early 19th century. And, as he most diligently maintained in *A Brief Inquiry into the True Nature and Character of Our Federal Government*, the true strength and assertiveness of the country depends upon the sovereign identity of the state. Only then, he wrote, will a people be able to defend themselves against the designs of an oppressive central power.

John Taylor (December 19, 1753 – August 21, 1824)

John Taylor (known as John Taylor of Caroline) was a seminal American political philosopher and statesman who played a crucial role in the development of Jeffersonian democracy. Orphaned as a child, Taylor was raised by his uncle, Edmund Pendleton, and received an education that included private tutoring and attendance at the College of William and Mary. He began his law studies under Pendleton's guidance, receiving his license in 1774. With the outbreak of the American Revolution, Taylor served in the Continental Army before joining the Virginia militia, eventually resigning in 1779.

Taylor's political career was marked by his service in the Virginia House of Delegates and three separate terms in the United States Senate (1792 – 94, 1803, 1822 – 24). Taylor was deeply involved in the political discourse of his time, being a staunch advocate for states' rights and a critic of centralized government. In fact, he even opposed the ratification of the Constitution due to fears of federal overreach. Nonetheless, he would soon unite with the author of the Constitution, James Madison. In response to the much-disputed Alien and Sedition Acts, he introduced James Madison's Virginia Resolutions to his state's legislature, expressing his unwavering devotion to individual liberty and limited government.

Beyond his political career, Taylor was a prolific writer, articulating his political philosophy in many books, such as *Arator* (1814), *An Inquiry into the Principles and Policy of the Government of the United States* (1814), and *Construction Construed and Constitutions Vindicated* (1820). These writings became the cornerstone of the Jeffersonian democratic ideology.

Even so, Taylor's legacy carries beyond the 1800s and into the present day. By emphasizing agrarian values, the sovereignty of the states, skepticism of centralized power, and a strict interpretation of the Constitution, he alerts any aspiring patriot to the dangers which constantly threaten and assail the banner of liberty.

A Note from the Editor

The following primary sources have been adjusted from their original manuscripts for easier readability. While the original grammar, capitalization, and typographic emphasis have been preserved, the spelling, punctuation, and page formatting have been modernized.

We have arranged the works according to what may best instruct the reader. Beginning with preliminary documents, each work builds upon the other to best establish the principles set out by its authors.

Additionally, you'll notice some works have two titles. In these cases, the second title is a representation of what it was in the original. This was done to remain faithful to the original works.

Please note, some insertions within the primary sources were made for convenience. These insertions, as implied, do not appear within their originals. To indicate such, additions will be enclosed with braces ("{" and "}"). The chapter headings in Upshur's work may be taken as an example.

Aside from these changes, the text remains unaltered.

We hope that these marvelous writings will inspire and illuminate your mind, guiding you to the true principles of American patriotism.

The Kentucky Resolutions

By Thomas Jefferson

---— 1799 ———

Kentucky Resolution – Alien and Sedition Acts

Resolutions in General Assembly

THE representatives of the good people of this commonwealth in general assembly convened, having maturely considered the answers of sundry states in the Union, to their resolutions passed at the last session, respecting certain unconstitutional laws of Congress, commonly called the alien and sedition laws, would be faithless indeed to themselves, and to those they represent, were they silently to acquiesce in principles and doctrines attempted to be maintained in all those answers, that of Virginia only excepted. To again enter the field of argument, and attempt more fully or forcibly to expose the unconstitutionality of those obnoxious laws, would, it is apprehended be as unnecessary as unavailing.

We cannot however but lament, that in the discussion of those interesting subjects, by sundry of the legislatures of our sister states, unfounded suggestions, and uncandid insinuations, derogatory of the true character and principles of the good people of this commonwealth, have been substituted in place of fair reasoning and sound argument. Our opinions of those alarming measures of the general government, together with our reasons for those opinions, were detailed with decency and with temper, and submitted to the discussion and judgment of our fellow citizens throughout the Union. Whether the decency and temper have been observed in the answers of most of those states who have denied or attempted to obviate the great truths contained in those resolutions, we have now only to submit to a candid world. Faithful to the true principles of the federal union, unconscious of any designs to disturb the harmony of that Union, and anxious only to escape the fangs of despotism, the good people of this commonwealth are regardless of censure or calumniation.

Least however the silence of this commonwealth should be construed into an acquiescence in the doctrines and principles advanced and attempted to be maintained by the said answers, or least those of our fellow citizens throughout the Union, who so widely differ from us on those important subjects, should be deluded by the expectation, that we shall be deterred from what we conceive our duty; or shrink from the principles contained in those resolutions: therefore.

RESOLVED, That this commonwealth considers the federal union, upon the terms and for the purposes specified in the late compact, as conducive to the liberty and happiness of the several states: That it does now unequivocally declare its attachment to the Union, and to that compact, agreeable to its obvious and real intention, and will be among the last to seek its dissolution: That if those who administer the general government be permitted to transgress the limits fixed by that compact, by a total disregard to the special delegations of power therein contained, annihilation of the state governments, and the erection upon their ruins, of a general consolidated government, will be the inevitable consequence: That the principle and construction contended for by sundry of the state legislatures, that the general government is the exclusive judge of the extent of the powers delegated to it, stop nothing short of despotism; since the discretion of those who administer the government, and not the constitution, would be the measure of their powers: That the several states who formed that instrument, being sovereign and independent, have the unquestionable right to judge of its infraction; and that a nullification, by those sovereignties, of all unauthorized acts done under color of that instrument, is the rightful remedy: That this commonwealth does upon the most deliberate reconsideration declare, that the said alien and sedition laws, are in their opinion, palpable violations of the said constitution; and however cheerfully it may be disposed to surrender its opinion to a majority of its sister states in matters of ordinary or doubtful policy; yet, in momentous regulations like the present, which so vitally wound the best rights of the citizen, it would consider a silent acquiescence as highly criminal: That although this commonwealth as a party to the federal compact; will bow to the laws of the Union, yet it does at the same time declare, that it will not now, nor ever hereafter, cease to oppose in a constitutional manner, every attempt from what quarter soever offered, to violate that compact:

AND FINALLY, in order that no pretexts or arguments may be drawn from a supposed acquiescence on the part of this commonwealth in the constitutionality of those laws, and be thereby used as precedents for similar future violations of federal compact; this commonwealth does now enter against them, its SOLEMN PROTEST.

Approved December 3rd, 1799.

The Virginia Resolutions

By James Madison

---- 1798 ----

VIRGINIA RESOLUTIONS

In the House of Delegates

Friday Dec. 21st. 1798.

RESOLVED, That the General Assembly of Virginia doth unequivocally express a firm resolution to maintain and defend the constitution of the United States, and the Constitution of this state, against every aggression, either foreign or domestic, and that they will support the government of the United States in all measures, warranted by the former.

That this Assembly most solemnly declares a warm attachment to the Union of the States, to maintain which, it pledges all its powers; and that for this end, it is their duty, to watch over and oppose every infraction of those principles, which constitute the only basis of that union, because a faithful observance of them, can alone secure its existence, and the public happiness.

That this Assembly doth explicitly and peremptorily declare, that it views the powers of the federal government, as resulting from the compact to which the states are parties; as limited by the plain sense and intention of the instrument constituting that compact; as no farther valid than they are authorized by the grants enumerated in that compact, and that in case of a deliberate, palpable, and dangerous exercise of other powers not granted by the said compact, the states who are parties thereto have the right, and are in duty bound, to interpose for arresting the progress of the evil, and for maintaining within their respective limits, the authorities, rights and liberties appertaining to them.

That the General Assembly doth also express its deep regret that a spirit has in sundry instances, been manifested by the federal government, to enlarge its powers by forced constructions of the constitutional charter which defines them; and that indications have appeared of a design to expound certain general phrases (which having been copied from the very limited grant of powers in the former articles of confederation were the less liable to be misconstrued) so as to destroy the meaning and effect of the particular enumeration, which necessarily explains and limits the general phrases; and so as to consolidate the states by degrees into one sovereignty, the obvious tendency and inevitable consequence of which would be, to transform the present republican system of the United States, into an absolute, or at best a mixed monarchy.

That the General Assembly doth particularly protest against the palpable and alarming infractions of the constitution, in the two late cases of the "alien and sedition acts," passed at the last session of Congress; the first of which exercises a power nowhere delegated to the federal government; and which by uniting legislative and judicial powers, to those of executive, subverts the general principles of free government, as well as the particular organization and positive provisions of the federal constitution: and the other of which acts, exercises in like manner a power not delegated by the constitution, but on the contrary, expressly and positively forbidden by one of the amendments thereto; a power, which more than any other ought to produce universal alarm, because it is levelled against that right of freely examining public characters and measures, and of free communication among the people thereon, which has ever been justly deemed, the only effectual guardian of every other right.

That this State having by its convention which ratified the federal constitution, expressly declared, "that among other essential rights, the liberty of conscience and of the Press cannot be cancelled, abridged, restrained or modified by any authority of the United States" and from its extreme anxiety to guard these rights from every possible attack of sophistry or ambition, having with other states recommended an amendment for that purpose, which amendment was in due time annexed to the Constitution, it would mark a reproachable inconsistency and criminal degeneracy, if an indifference were now shewn to the most palpable violation of one of the Rights thus declared and secured, and to the establishment of a precedent which may be fatal to the other.

That the good people of this Commonwealth, having ever felt and continuing to feel, the most sincere affection for their brethren of the other states, the truest anxiety for establishing and perpetuating the union of all, and the most scrupulous fidelity to that Constitution which is the pledge of mutual friendship, and the instrument of mutual happiness, the General Assembly doth solemnly appeal to the like dispositions of the other States, in confidence that they will concur with this Commonwealth in declaring, as it does hereby declare, that the acts aforesaid are unconstitutional, and that the necessary and proper measures will be taken by each, for cooperating with this State in maintaining unimpaired the authorities, rights, and liberties, reserved to the States respectively, or to the people.

That the Governor be desired to transmit a copy of the foregoing Resolutions to the Executive authority of each of the other States, with a request, that the same may be communicated to the Legislature thereof.

And that a copy be furnished to each of the Senators and Representatives, representing this State in the Congress of the United States.

"Report of 1800"

By James Madison

──────── 1800 ────────

James Madison

Report on the Virginia Resolutions

House of Delegates, Session of 1799 – 1800

Report of the Committee to whom were referred the Communications of various States, relative to the Resolutions of the last General Assembly of this State, concerning the Alien and Sedition Laws.

Whatever room might be found in the proceedings of some of the states, who have disapproved of the resolutions of the General Assembly of this commonwealth, passed on the 21st day of December, 1798, for painful remarks on the spirit and manner of those proceedings, it appears to the committee most consistent with the duty, as well as dignity, of the General Assembly, to hasten an oblivion of every circumstance which might be construed into a diminution of mutual respect, confidence, and affection, among the members of the Union.

The committee have deemed it a more useful task to revise, with a critical eye, the resolutions which have met with their disapprobation; to examine fully the several objections and arguments which have appeared against them; and to inquire whether there be any errors of fact, of principle, or of reasoning, which the candor of the General Assembly ought to acknowledge and correct.

The *first* of the resolutions is in the words following: –

> *Resolved*, That the General Assembly of Virginia doth unequivocally express a firm resolution to maintain and defend the Constitution of the United States, and the Constitution of this state, against every aggression, either foreign or domestic; and that they will support the government of the United States in all measures warranted by the former.

No unfavorable comment can have been made on the sentiments

here expressed. To maintain and defend the Constitution of the United States, and of their own state, against every aggression, both foreign and domestic, and to support the government of the United States in all measures warranted by their Constitution, are duties which the General Assembly ought always to feel, and to which, on such an occasion, it was evidently proper to express their sincere and firm adherence.

In their *next* resolution –

> The General Assembly most solemnly declares a warm attachment to the union of the states, to maintain which it pledges all its powers; and that, for this end, it is their duty to watch over and oppose every infraction of those principles which constitute the only basis of that Union, because a faithful observance of them can alone secure its existence and the public happiness.

The observation just made is equally applicable to this solemn declaration of warm attachment to the Union, and this solemn pledge to maintain it; nor can any question arise among enlightened friends of the Union, as to the duty of watching over and opposing every infraction of those principles which constitute its basis, and a faithful observance of which can alone secure its existence, and the public happiness thereon depending.

The *third* resolution is in the words following: –

> That this Assembly doth explicitly and peremptorily declare, that it views the powers of the federal government, as resulting from the compact to which the states are parties, as limited by the plain sense and intention of the instrument constituting that compact – as no further valid than they are authorized by the grants enumerated in that compact; and that, in case of a deliberate, palpable, and dangerous exercise of other powers, not granted by the said compact, the states who are parties thereto have the right, and are in duty bound, to interpose, for arresting the progress of the evil and for maintaining, within

their respective limits, the authorities, rights, and liberties appertaining to them.

On this resolution the committee have bestowed all the attention which its importance merits. They have *scanned* it not merely with a strict, but with a severe eye; and they feel confidence in pronouncing that, in its just and fair construction, it is unexceptionably true in its several positions, as well as constitutional and conclusive in its inferences.

The resolution declares, *first*, that "it views the powers of the federal government as resulting from the compact to which the states are parties"; in other words, that the federal powers are derived from the Constitution; and that the Constitution is a compact to which the states are parties.

Clear as the position must seem, that the federal powers are derived from the Constitution, and from that alone, the committee are not unapprised of a late doctrine which opens another source of federal powers, not less extensive and important than it is new and unexpected. The examination of this doctrine will be most conveniently connected with a review of a succeeding resolution. The committee satisfy themselves here with briefly remarking that, in all the contemporary discussions and comments which the Constitution underwent, it was constantly justified and recommended on the ground that the powers not given to the government were withheld from it; and that, if any doubt could have existed on this subject, under the original text of the Constitution, it is removed, as far as words could remove it, by the 12th amendment, now a part of the Constitution, {which is now the 10th amendment,} which expressly declares, "that the powers not delegated to the United States by the Constitution, nor prohibited by it to the states, are reserved to the states respectively, or to the people."

The other position involved in this branch of the resolution, namely, "that the states are parties to the Constitution," or compact, is, in the judgment of the committee, equally free from objection. It is indeed true that the term "states" is sometimes used in a vague sense, and sometimes in different senses, according to the subject to which it is applied. Thus it sometimes means the separate sections of territory occupied by the political societies within each; sometimes the particular governments established by those societies; sometimes those societies as organized into those particular governments; and lastly, it means the people composing those political societies, in their highest sovereign capacity. Although it might be wished that the perfection of language admitted less diversity in the signification of the same words, yet little inconvenience is produced by it, where the true sense can be collected with certainty from the different applications. In the present instance, whatever different construction of the term "states," in the resolution, may have been entertained, all will at least concur in that last mentioned; because in that sense the Constitution was submitted to the "states"; in that sense the "states" ratified it; and in that sense of the term "states," they are consequently parties to the compact from which the powers of the federal government result.

The next position is, that the General Assembly views the powers of the federal government "as limited by the plain sense and intention of the instrument constituting that compact," and "as no further valid than they are authorized by the grants therein enumerated." It does not seem possible that any just objection can lie against either of these clauses. The first amounts merely to a declaration that the compact ought to have the interpretation plainly intended by the parties to it; the other, to a declaration that it ought to have the execution and effect intended by them. If the powers granted be valid, it is solely because they are granted; and if the granted powers are valid because granted, all other powers not granted must not be valid.

The resolution, having taken this view of the federal compact, proceeds to infer, "That, in case of a deliberate, palpable, and dangerous exercise of other powers, not granted by the said compact, the states, who are parties thereto, have the right, and are in duty bound, to interpose for arresting the progress of the evil, and for maintaining, within their respective limits, the authorities, rights, and liberties, appertaining to them."

It appears to your committee to be a plain principle, founded in common sense, illustrated by common practice, and essential to the nature of compacts, that, where resort can be had to no tribunal superior to the authority of the parties, the parties themselves must be the rightful judges, in the last resort, whether the bargain made has been pursued or violated. The Constitution of the United States was formed by the sanction of the states, given by each in its sovereign capacity. It adds to the stability and dignity, as well as to the authority, of the Constitution, that it rests on this legitimate and solid foundation. The states, then, being the parties to the constitutional compact, and in their sovereign capacity, it follows of necessity that there can be no tribunal, above their authority, to decide, in the last resort, whether the compact made by them be violated; and consequently, that, as the parties to it, they must themselves decide, in the last resort, such questions as may be of sufficient magnitude to require their interposition.

It does not follow, however, because the states, as sovereign parties to their constitutional compact, must ultimately decide whether it has been violated, that such a decision ought to be interposed either in a hasty manner or on doubtful and inferior occasions. Even in the case of ordinary conventions between different nations, where, by the strict rule of interpretation, a breach of a part may be deemed a breach of the whole – every part being deemed a condition of every other part, and of the whole – it is always laid down that the breach must be both willful and material, to justify an application of the rule. But in the case of an intimate and constitutional union, like that of the United States, it is evident that the interposition of the parties, in their sovereign capacity, can be called for by occasions only deeply and essentially affecting the vital principles of their political system.

The resolution has, accordingly guarded against any misapprehension of its object, by expressly requiring, for such an interposition, "the case of a deliberate, palpable, and dangerous breach of the Constitution, by the exercise of powers not granted by it." It must be a case not of a light and transient nature, but of a nature dangerous to the great purposes for which the Constitution was established. It must be a case, moreover, not obscure or doubtful in its construction, but plain and palpable. Lastly, it must be a case not resulting from a partial consideration or hasty determination; but a case stamped with a final consideration and deliberate adherence. It is not necessary, because the resolution does not require, that the question should be discussed, how far the exercise of any particular power, ungranted by the Constitution, would justify the interposition of the parties to it. As cases might easily be stated, which none would contend ought to fall within that description – cases, on the other hand, might, with equal ease, be stated, so flagrant and so fatal as to unite every opinion in placing them within the description.

But the resolution has done more than guard against misconstruction, by expressly referring to cases of a deliberate, palpable, and dangerous nature. It specifies the object of the interposition, which it contemplates to be solely that of arresting the progress of the evil of usurpation, and of maintaining the authorities, rights, and liberties appertaining to the states as parties to the Constitution.

From this view of the resolution, it would seem inconceivable that it can incur any just disapprobation from those who, laying aside all momentary impressions, and recollecting the genuine source and object of the Federal Constitution, shall candidly and accurately interpret the meaning of the General Assembly. If the deliberate exercise of dangerous powers, palpably withheld by the Constitution, could not justify the parties to it in interposing even so far as to arrest the progress of the evil, and thereby to preserve the Constitution itself, as well as to provide for the safety of the parties to it; there would be an end to all relief from usurped power, and a direct subversion of the rights specified or recognized under all the state constitutions, as well as a plain denial of the fundamental principle on which our independence itself was declared.

But it is objected, that the judicial authority is to be regarded as the sole expositor of the Constitution in the last resort; and it may be asked for what reason the declaration by the General Assembly, supposing it to be theoretically true, could be required at the present day, and in so solemn a manner.

On this objection it might be observed, first, that there may be instances of usurped power, which the forms of the Constitution would never draw within the control of the judicial department; secondly, that, if the decision of the judiciary be raised above the authority of the sovereign parties to the Constitution, the decisions of the other departments, not carried by the forms of the Constitution before the judiciary, must be equally authoritative and final with the decisions of that department. But the proper answer to the objection is, that the resolution of the General Assembly relates to those great and extraordinary cases, in which all the forms of the Constitution may prove ineffectual against infractions dangerous to the essential rights of the parties to it. The resolution supposes that dangerous powers, not delegated, may not only be usurped and executed by the other departments, but that the judicial department, also, may exercise or sanction dangerous powers beyond the grant of the Constitution; and, consequently, that the ultimate right of the parties to the Constitution, to judge whether the compact has been dangerously violated, must extend to violations by one delegated authority as well as by another – by the judiciary as well as by the executive, or the legislature.

However true, therefore, it may be, that the judicial department is, in all questions submitted to it by the forms of the Constitution, to decide in the last resort, this resort must necessarily be deemed the last in relation to the authorities of the other departments of the government; not in relation to the rights of the parties to the constitutional compact, from which the judicial, as well as the other departments, hold their delegated trusts. On any other hypothesis, the delegation of judicial power would annul the authority delegating it; and the concurrence of this department with the others in usurped powers, might subvert forever, and beyond the possible reach of any rightful remedy, the very Constitution which all were instituted to preserve.

The truth declared in the resolution being established, the expediency of making the declaration at the present day may safely be left to the temperate consideration and candid judgment of the American public. It will be remembered, that a frequent recurrence to fundamental principles is solemnly enjoined by most of the state constitutions, and particularly by our own, as a necessary safeguard against the danger of degeneracy, to which republics are liable, as well as other governments, though in a less degree than others. And a fair comparison of the political doctrines not infrequent at the present day, with those which characterized the epoch of our revolution, and which form the basis of our republican constitutions, will best determine whether the declaratory recurrence here made to those principles ought to be viewed as unseasonable and improper, or as a vigilant discharge of an important duty. The authority of constitutions over governments, and of the sovereignty of the people over constitutions, are truths which are at all times necessary to be kept in mind; and at no time, perhaps, more necessary than at present.

These observations appear to form a satisfactory reply to every objection which is not founded on a misconception of the terms employed in the resolutions. There is one other, however, which may be of too much importance not to be added. It cannot be forgotten that, among the arguments addressed to those who apprehended danger to liberty from the establishment of the general government over so great a country, the appeal was emphatically made to the intermediate existence of the state governments between the people and that government, to the vigilance with which they would descry the first symptoms of usurpation, and to the promptitude with which they would sound the alarm to the public. This argument was probably not without its effect; and if it was a proper one then to recommend the establishment of a constitution; it must be a proper one now to assist in its interpretation.*

---

* These observations appear to form a satisfactory reply to every objection which is not founded on a misconception of the terms employed in the resolutions. There is one other, however, which may be of too much importance not to be added. It cannot be forgotten that, among the arguments addressed to those who apprehended danger to liberty from the establishment of the general government over so great a country, the appeal was emphatically made to the intermediate existence of the state governments between the people and that government, to the vigilance with which they would descry the first symptoms of usurpation, and to the promptitude with which they would sound the alarm to the public. This argument was probably not without its effect; and if it was a proper one then to recommend the establishment of a constitution; it must be a proper one now to assist in its interpretation.

A Political Catechism

By Maria Pinckney

1830

THE QUINTESSENSE OF LONG SPEECHES ARRANGED AS A POLITICAL CATECHISM:

BY A LADY FOR HER GOD-DAUGHTER

A Political Catechism

Question – What do we understand by the Federal Union?

Answer – It is an agreement between Sovereign States, to forbear exerting their sovereign power over certain defined objects, and to exert jointly their sovereign power over other specified objects, through the agency of a General Government. Each State agrees to exert its full sovereign power jointly, for all external purposes; and separately, for all internal purposes, or State concerns.

Q. Where is this Agreement found?

A. In the bond of Union, or compact between the States, called the Federal Constitution.

Q. What is the nature of the Federal Constitution?

A. It is a compact based upon cautious and jealous specifications. The distinguished body of men who framed it, guarded and defined every power that was to be exercised through the agency of the General Government – and every other power not enumerated in the compact, was to be reserved and exercised by the States.

Q. Did the States, in forming the Constitution, divest themselves of any part of their Sovereignty?

A. Of not a particle. The individuality and sovereign personality of the States was not at all impaired. The States agreed, by the Constitution, that they would unite in exerting their powers, therein specified and defined, for the purpose and objects therein designated, and through the agency of the machinery therein created; but the power exercised by the functionaries of the General Government, is not *inherent* in them, but in the States whose agents they are. The Constitution is their Power of Attorney, to do certain acts; and contains, connected with their authority to act, their letter of instruction, as to the manner in which they shall act. They are the Servants. The power which gives validity to their acts is in their Masters – THE STATES.

Q. Where is the power of Congress during the recess of that body?

A. It possesses no sovereign power – it is but the agent of the Sovereign States.

Q. Can you illustrate this retention of Sovereignty by the States by any other example?

A. Suppose an individual, for instance, was to stipulate to transact a portion of his business by an agent, and the remainder by himself, and to forbear to exert his moral faculties, and physical energies upon that class of subjects, which, by his agreement, are to be acted upon by his agent. Has he by his stipulation lessened, impaired, or diminished his moral or physical powers? On the contrary, the validity of the agency depends upon his retaining those faculties, for if he shall become insane, or die, the agent cannot act, because the power of his principal has become extinct; so it is the power, the full subsisting Sovereign Power of the States, which gives validity to the acts of the General Government. The validity of these acts does not result from the exercise of a portion of the Sovereign Power of each State.

Q. Why then has it been supposed by some, that when the States formed the Constitution, they cut the Sovereignty of each State into two parts, and gave much the larger portion to the General Government?

A. Many erroneous and mischievous opinions proceed from ignorance of the true meaning of words. Sovereignty, Rebellion, Nullification, &c. we hear every day used, without any precise idea being attached to their signification.

Q. What is the meaning of Sovereignty?

A. It is the will of civil society in the Social Compact, which society is a moral person, whose will, like the will of the human being, cannot be divided without destroying the person; we can conceive the will operating in a thousand various ways, but we cannot conceive its separation into parts; neither can we conceive of the separation of Sovereignty – its unity and life are inseparable.

Q. How do you define Rebellion?

A. It is the resistance of an *inferior* to the lawful authority of a *superior.* A child may rebel against a parent – a slave against his master – citizens against the government, and colonies against the mother-country – but a State cannot rebel; because one Sovereign cannot rebel against another, for all Sovereigns are equal. The Sovereignty of the little State of Delaware is equal to that of New-York, or of Russia, though the physical power of those Sovereignties are vastly different. The supposition, therefore, that a Sovereign State can commit Rebellion,[*] Treason, or any crime whatever, is utterly inadmissible in the science of politics. The idea of crime cannot exist where there is no conceivable or possible tribunal, before which the culprit could be arraigned and convicted. Still less can any State be supposed to incur the guilt of rebellion or treason, by resisting an unconstitutional law of the General Government. The General Government is the creature of the States – the offspring of their Sovereign Power. Is the Creator to be governed by the lawless authority of the Creature? We cannot invert the rule of reason and of law upon that subject, and say, that the superior incurs guilt by resisting the inferior, and not the inferior by resisting the superior.

Q. What is the meaning of Nullification?

A. It is the veto[**] of a Sovereign State on an unconstitutional law of Congress.

Q. Are not unconstitutional laws, of course, null and void?

---

[*] *Rebel.* — Was a State Government to nullify even a *Constitutional* law of Congress, it could not place the State (that is the people of the State) in an attitude of rebellion; if war ensues, it is one government warring against another, as England against France, &c. The essence of Rebellion is inferiority.

[**] *Veto.* — A writer in one of the Gazettes says, that Veto is suspensive and Nullification is destructive. It is to be hoped that the late Veto of the President was not meant to be suspensive, but will prove altogether destructive.

A. Undoubtedly; and an act of Usurpation is not obligatory; it is not law, and resistance is justifiable. In virtue of her Sovereignty, the State is the judge of her own rights, and bound as Sovereign to protect her citizens, which she does by nullifying* the obnoxious law, and releasing them from any obligation to obey it.

Q. Has not this right of the State been denied?

A. Only by those who are enemies of State Rights, whose subterfuge is, that they can find Nullification nowhere in the Constitution. Suppose a State was to make a treaty with a foreign government, to coin money, to grant letters of marque, or assume any power that she had by the compact delegated to the General Government. When Congress should nullify the assumption, would the State have any right to complain that she could not find Nullification in the Constitution? If the implied right is reciprocal, the State possesses the double right to Nullify, for all rights are reserved to her, that are not specified in the Constitution.

Q. Is there no other check upon the General Government, than the one just mentioned of Nullification?

A. The oath, the several legislative, executive and judicial officers of the several States take to support the Federal Constitution, ought to be as effectual security against the usurpation of the General Government, as it is against the encroachments of the State Governments. For the increase of the powers by usurpation, is as clearly a violation of the Federal Constitution, as a diminution of these powers by private encroachments; and that oath obliges the

---

* *Nullifying.* — It is contended that the Kentucky and Virginia Resolutions, which confirm the right of Nullification, in cases of a palpable, deliberate, and dangerous usurpation of power, speak of resistance by the mode pointed out in them, always in the plural number. That it is the States which are bound to interpose; and that, consequently, a State, being in the singular number cannot interfere and act individually. This is a mere evasion of the enemies of State Rights; for example: If it were said that the submission or alarm-men were permitted to reveal the secret, by which the heterogenous, spurious party obtained the late victory; is it inferred that they are all to assemble together to avail themselves of the permission, and that one alarmist, being in the singular number, cannot, individually, divulge it? It is the individuality and sovereign personality of the State which confers the right of Nullification.

officers of the several States as vigorously to oppose the one as the other.

Q. Could then any collision arise between the States and the Federal Government, were each confined to its proper sphere?

A. The Constitution has left them sufficient space to move harmoniously together; but it is the General Government that is continually wandering out of the sphere of its legitimacy, and usurping powers, that the combined wisdom of the States imagined, they had carefully guarded from all encroachments.

Q. Have the States ever resumed any of the powers they have delegated to the General Government?

A. Never, in a single instance, have they violated, or attempted to violate the Constitution. The enemies of State Rights pretend, that had the States the right to judge of an unconstitutional law of Congress, (in other words, of an infringement on their Sovereignty) they would transcend their appropriate sphere, and usurp* the powers assigned to the General Government. On the contrary, it is not the interest of the States to resume the powers they have delegated. The same motives which led to the formation of the Union, a conviction of its utility, are as strong now that its beneficial effects have been experienced, as when they were only anticipated. They have evinced from the period of its formation, no sentiment so strong, as an ardent and devoted attachment to the Union. In Union, they take their high station among the nations of the earth; and in Union, the Star-Spangled Banner waves over every sea. But there is a principle we should never forget, that the greatest good when perverted becomes the greatest evil. The Union as it was formed – an Union of Free, Sovereign and Independent States – an Union, affording equal protection and mutual benefit to all, will be considered the greatest political good; but as highly as it ought to be valued, it is not the

---

* *Usurp.* — All power to govern is delegated or usurped. The delegated power may *Usurp* other powers not delegated, but the power that delegates cannot *Usurp*, it *resumes* the power it has delegated — delegated power is trust. The Trustees, therefore, that is the General Government, *Usurp*. The States, who granted the trust, *resume*.

greatest possible good. There is one still better – still more precious – one which is prized infinitely higher – it is LIBERTY – that LIBERTY for which our Fathers toiled and bled. The usurpations and tyranny of Great Britain were not resisted, that the COLONIES might be UNITED, but that the COLONIES might be FREE, and for the PEOPLE to be FREE, the STATES must be FREE. Whenever the States cease to maintain their Sovereignty unimpaired, and become vassals of the General Government, the duration of the Union will then, indeed, be problematical. It is, therefore, on the friends of the State Rights – on the supporters of State Rights – on those who cling to State Rights, as to the palladium of their liberties, that we must rely for the maintenance and perpetuity of the Union, and not on the enemies of State Rights.* The weak – the timid – the apathetic, and the ambitious, who raise the cry of disunion to palsy the unity of action, that would emancipate us from the chains of usurpation – these are the real disunionists, and to these and these *only*, will be attributed, the evils arising from the dissolution of the Union.

Q. What is the new version of the Constitution by Messrs. Webster & Co.?

A. They have discovered that the Constitution was not formed by the States in their Sovereign capacity – that it is not a compact between the States – but that it is a Government formed by the people, *en masse*, that is, by the people collected into one nation – that this nation brought the Government into existence – established it, and hath hitherto supported it for the very purpose, among others, of imposing certain salutary restraints on State Sovereignties. That in forming this National Government, the people conferred upon the Supreme Court, the power of imposing these certain salutary restraints upon the Sovereignty of the States.

---

* *State Rights.* — There is a test by which the real State Right Party may at once be distinguished from the counterfeit, who assume their name to conquer under false colors. The real State Right Party hold as their Cardinal Doctrine that, as guardian of its reserved rights, each State is the judge for itself, of an infringement of them; that there is, under the Union, a peaceable mode of redress, when the Constitution has been violated, and that every State is bound by a political necessity to maintain its Sovereignty unimpaired, as essential to the liberty of the people, and preservation of the Union.

Q. To what do these Doctrines lead?

A. To the annihilation of State Rights, and consequently, of the fundamental principles of Constitutional Liberty, for which our Fathers fought and conquered.

Q. How did they contrive to convert the people of thirteen distinct States into one people?

A. A short analysis of the process by which a State is formed, will demonstrate the impossibility. The discussion of the elements of Government is dull, as is all abstract discussion. But if we undertake to talk politics, we must undertake to know about what we talk, and we cannot understand the nature of our Government, without referring to first principles.

Q. By what process are States formed?

A. There are but two conditions of mankind – the one national, and the other artificial. In a state of nature, there is no government. The laws of nature are the only rules of human conduct, and each individual is his own expounder of those laws. He is the arbiter of his own rights, and the avenger of his own wrongs. There is no power (that is, no moral power) in one man to direct, control, or govern another; all are equally free. The evils inseparable from this condition, induce those who are suffering from it to escape to the artificial state. The transition from a state of nature to that of civil society, is effected by an agreement among all who compose the society, that each and his concerns, shall be directed by the understanding, and protected by the power of all. The agreement is reciprocal. The right which each man possessed, in a state of nature, to direct himself, is voluntarily surrendered by him to the society, and he agrees, that he and his concerns shall henceforth be subject to the will of the society. This contract is either expressed or understood. The power to govern can be obtained upon no other supposition. It is denominated the social compact. It is the charter by which civil society is incorporated, by which it acquires personality and unity; by which the action of all the people, is considered as the action of a moral agent, of a single person. This moral agent is, in reference to its own condition, called a state, probably, from the fixed and stable condition of the people, compared with their unstable and fluctuating condition in a state of nature. The people compressed or compacted by the social compact into the unit, called a State, remains unchanged under all the changes of its Government, which accident may produce, or war or convulsion may inflict. If a Republic becomes a Monarchy, or a Monarchy a Republic, or if compacts are formed with other States, these are but changes of Government, the Civil Society or State remains unchanged, and is Sovereign, while ever it manages its own affairs by its own will. It is upon this principle that States are not absolved from their debts by revolution. The State and not the Government is the contracting party, and nothing but the dissolution of the social compact and consequent extinction of the State, can absolve it from its payment. Much confusion has arisen from the indiscriminate use of the word State. State means the people in their political capacity, and never their government. By this reference to first principles, we find from the existing state of things – as there were thirteen distinct States at the time the Constitution was formed – that it must of necessity have been formed by the States, not by the people consolidated into one nation, for in no other way could they have been collected into one, but by first absolving themselves from their allegiance to their respective States, and dissolving the compacts by which they were formed into States. Civil Societies have been destroyed by earthquakes, by deluge, and by the exterminating ravages of war; they have often been subdued into vassalage or reduced by usurpation to the condition of the provinces, but we have no account in history of a people voluntarily dissolving the social compact. Messrs. Webster & Co's. discovery, therefore, is a proof that there is no absurdity too great for those who are determined to accomplish their views on particular subjects.

Q. Does not the Supreme Court also contend that the Constitution was formed by the people, collectively?

A. The Supreme Court is the creature of the General Government, and has with a constancy and silence, like the approaches of death, adhered to a construction that has increased its own power – enlarged that of the General Government, and thrown chains over State Rights – chains never dreamed of at the formation of the Constitution.

Q. Upon what does the Supreme Court and Messrs. Webster & Co. found their discovery?

A. Upon the preamble to the Constitution – it is in these words: "We the people of the United States, to form a more perfect Union," &c.

To people of common understanding, black actually means black, and white really white; but to Messrs. Webster & Co. it means just the reverse. "We the people of the United States" means according to them – "We the people *not* of the United States, but the people collectively."

Q. When the States formed the Constitution, under which kind of government were they?

A. They were united by the Confederation. To form a more perfect Union of the States already united, to consolidate their Union, was the object of the present Constitution, and not to unite the people, for it was impossible to unite them more perfectly by a Constitution than they were already united by the social compact.

Q. What is the nature of the Supreme Court, that according to Messrs. Webster & Co. has the power of imposing salutary restraints upon State Sovereignty?

A. The epithet of supreme which gives importance to the Court and imposes on the ignorant, is entirely relative, and imports only that appellative jurisdiction which it may exercise over the subordinate Courts of the *General Government.* The appellative Court, or Court of Appeals of every State, is just as supreme for the same reason – it also exercises jurisdiction over the inferior Courts. It is not called supreme, in reference to the other departments of the

Government, nor has it any supremacy in reference to the States. The power accorded it is *purely judicial*. It is the umpire in all cases of law and equity arising under the Constitution. But questions of sovereignty, policy, or expediency, are unsusceptible of its judicial cognizance and decision. The power to declare a law of Congress, or any of the States, unconstitutional, was never intended to be conferred on the Supreme Court as a *direct* power. The exercise of the power is merely *incidental* in exercising the judicial power. The Constitutionality of a law may be *incidentally* decided, in deciding the law and justice of a case. But the decision must be given in the exercise of merely judicial, and not of political power. Can it be believed that the great men who framed the Constitution, and guarded each specification with such zealous care, ever intended to subject the whole to the control of a judicial Oligarchy? The power asserted for the Supreme Court, is superior to that of imperial Rome in her proudest days. The conquests of Rome were achieved at an incalculable expense of blood and treasure. But the Supreme Court may vassal twenty-four Sovereign States, without expending one cent or shedding one drop of blood.

If the States were but true to themselves, and faithful in the discharge of their high duties, they would move on in the majesty of their sovereign power, and maintain with a steady and equal hand both their Governments within its appropriate sphere, and not permit the mere modicum of judicial power which they have granted to the Supreme Court, to control them in the exercise of their sovereign power.

Q. Why have the States allowed the Constitution, the sacred legacy of the combined wisdom of their fathers, to be violated by sacrilegious hands?

A. Because that self-interest is the governing principle of three-fourths of mankind. The North, East, and West acquiesced in the usurpation of the General Government, because it was for their exclusive benefit, while the South was passive through apathy and sleep. The North and East bribed the West by internal improvement, and by donations of the public lands – and the West in her turn, bribed the North and East with the Tariff. Internal improvement and a Tariff of protection, are twin born abominations unknown to the Constitution. The South, whose vital interests and almost her existence depended on the inviolability of the Constitution, scarcely awakened from her dream of sovereignty, finds herself the vassal province of a *Consolidated Central Government*, without limitation to its power, but the will of the majority to legislate for the general welfare – the very government by usurpation, that the Supreme Court and Messrs. Webster &. Co. discovered was established by the people. The usurped power is a virtual abrogation of the Constitution, and consequently leaves the minority to ruin and degradation. This minority is the South.

Q. What is the remedy for these evils, according to the submission men, [or Tories of the Revolution?]

A. To shut our eyes – hold our tongues, and fold our arms.

Q. What is the greatest anomaly at present in the Union?

A. It is, that the South, whose *beau ideal* was LIBERTY, who sacrificed to it as to the God of their idolatry, is now in vassalage to the North, East and West.

Q. To what may the patriotism of many here be likened?

A. To the philanthropists, whose charity is too exalted to relieve the misery at their own door, but are willing to bestow it on three-quarters of the globe.

Q. What is the feeling that Carolina's real sons cherish for her at this moment?

A. That feeling so touchingly and beautifully expressed by the Beaufort Orator on the last anniversary of independence. "If, in celebrations like this, the name of Carolina was unmentioned by her Orators, the omission was altogether unmarked – why was it when now you can think only of her? It was, because she had not yet been depressed into notorious inequality from the level of the majority of her Sister States. She was not yet in full possession of that deepest and most touching attractiveness, with which misfortune and the world's persecution never fail to invest a beloved object in the contemplation of the generous and brave; you had not yet felt in the cold and cutting blast of federal unkindness the necessity of cherishing and warming her in your hearts. She had been prosperous and affluent, and you but rejoiced that she was your State – she had been honored – and you were but proud of her, as your section of the Union; but when she was injured and insulted, we felt that she was our country! And when she was most insolently trampled, we clung to her most fondly, and when they called her weakest, our hearts beat strongest in her cause."

Q. What is the attitude Carolina should assume at the present crisis?

A. She must at once appeal to her sovereignty, and decide whether she shall herself exert the protecting power of Nullification through the organs of her Legislature, or assuming her highest attitude of sovereignty, through that of a Convention.

Q. What will be the result of this resistance on the part of the State to the obnoxious usurpation?

A. The first result will be, the preservation of her sovereignty – the next result, the General Government, no longer relying on the supineness of the State, will be driven back to the sphere of its legitimacy.

Q. But if one of these results should not follow, must the State forbear to resist the aggression upon her rights?

A. No – decidedly no. She must maintain her sovereignty at every hazard, and every means within her power. She is good for nothing – worse than good for nothing – without it.

Q. Will this not lead to civil war – to war between the State, and the General Government?

A. No: The General Government would not put itself so completely in the wrong, as to consecrate its Usurpation by the blood of those it shall have attempted to oppress. If the State is led by apprehensions of this kind to submit to oppression, there is then an end of shaking off her fetters. Fear is a bad counsellor of even an individual, it should never be consulted by a Sovereign State. The strength and powers of Usurpation consist wholly in the fear of resisting it. Let the State only will to be free, and the General Government must recede from its pretensions.

Q. But if the General Government does not recede?

A. Then let the State send a solemn embassy to the bar of Congress, and demand as a Sovereign State, one of the parties to the compact, a redress of her grievances, or an appeal to the ultimate arbiter, provided by the fifth article in the Constitution. Three-fourths of the States compose this august tribunal.[*] The State does not compromise her dignity, by referring to them questions of Sovereignty being themselves Sovereign, but she cannot without violating every principle of self-respect, submit a question in relation to her sovereignty to one of her subalterns, the Supreme Court. It is in the power of this tribunal to define anew the relations between the State and the General Government; if it does not concur in admitting the contested power, or shall not pronounce that it already exists, the General Government will at once be constrained to abandon the exercise of it, for no new power could have been granted without the concurrence of this tribunal.

Q. But if three-fourths of the States, the ultimate arbiter, decide the question against the State, whose vital interest is at stake, does acquiescence become a duty?

A. The State must then calculate the value of the Union; she has

---

[*] *Three-fourths.* — It has been said in a late State Paper, that the States by assenting to the provision of the Constitution, that three-fourths of them might amend or change it, surrendered individually their original Sovereignty, and that the Sovereignty of the Union actually now resides in three-fourths of them. This is an erroneous opinion. The States agreed that the voice of all should be expressed by three-fourths, there was no surrender of individual Sovereignty.

always the right of secession, but we will not, even in idea, "fathom the abyss, until we have descended the precipice of disunion."

Q. On whom must Carolina depend in her hour of peril?

A. On the descendants of the patriot band who achieved the Revolution. On the descendants of those brave and generous foreigners who united with us in that arduous and glorious struggle. On the proprietors of the soil – and on those whose motto is "MILLIONS FOR DEFENCE, NOT A CENT FOR TRIBUTE."

"The Danger Not Over"

From the Richmond *Examiner*, October 1801,

By Edmund Pendleton

---- 1801 ----

The Danger Not Over

Although one of my age can have little to hope, and less to fear, from forms of government, as rather belonging to the next world, than the present, and possibly may be charged with intermeddling where he has no interest whenever he utters opinions concerning social regulations, yet I feel impelled by an anxious desire to promote the happiness of my country to submit to the public consideration some reflections on our present political state.

It is far from my intention to damp the public joy occasioned by the late changes of our public agents or to disturb the calm that already presages the most beneficial consequences. On the contrary, I consider this event as having arrested a train of measures that were gradually conducting us towards ruin.

These changes will be a matter of tenfold congratulation if we make the proper use of them. If, instead of negligently reposing upon that wisdom and integrity which have already softened even political malice, we seize an opportunity to erect new barriers against folly, fraud, and ambition; and to explain such parts of the Constitution as have been already, or may be, interpreted contrary to the intention of those who adopted it.

This proposition does not argue a want of proper confidence in our present Chief Magistrate, but the contrary. It can be no censure to believe that he has a nobler destiny to fulfill than that of making his contemporary countrymen happy for a few years, and that the rare event of such a character at the head of a nation imposes on us the sacred duty of seizing the propitious opportunity to do all in our power to perpetuate that happiness. As to that species of confidence that would extinguish free inquiry and popular watchfulness, it is never desired by patriotism nor ought to be yielded by freemen.

In pursuit of our purpose, we ought to keep in mind certain principles which are believed to be sound; to enquire whether they have been violated under the Constitution; and then consider how a repetition of those violations may be prevented. As thus:

1. Government is instituted for the good of the community and not to gratify avarice or ambition; therefore, unnecessary increase of debt – appointment of useless officers such as stationary ministers to foreign courts with which we have little connection and 16 additional judges at a time when the business of the federal courts had greatly diminished – and engaging us in a war abroad for the sake of advancing party projects at home, are abuses in government.

2. The chief good derivable from government is *civil liberty*, and if government is so constructed as to enable its administration to assail that liberty with the several weapons heretofore most fatal to it, the structure is defective. Of this sort, standing armies, fleets, severe penal laws, war, and a multitude of civil officers, are universally admitted to be; and if our government can, with ease and impunity, array those forces against social liberty, the Constitution is defective.

3. Peace is undoubtedly that state which proposes to society the best chance for the continuance of freedom and happiness, and the situation of America is such as to expose her to fewer occasions for war than any other nation, whilst it also disables her from gaining anything by war. But if, by indirect means, the executive can involve us in war not declared by the legislature; if a treaty may be made which will incidentally produce a war, and the legislature are bound to pass all laws necessary to give it full effect; or if the judiciary may determine a war to exist although the legislature hath refused to declare it; then the Constitution is defective, since it admits constructions which pawn our freedom and happiness upon the security of executive patriotism, which is inconsistent with republican principles.

4. Union is certainly the basis of our political prosperity, and this can only be preserved by confining, with precision, the federal government to the exercise of powers clearly required by the general interest or respecting foreign nations and the

state governments to objects of a local nature; because the states exhibit such varieties of character and interests that a consolidated general government would be in a perpetual conflict with state interests, from its want of local knowledge or from a prevalence of local prejudice or interest, so as certainly to produce civil war and disunion.

If, then, the distinct provinces of the general and state governments are not clearly defined; if the former may assail the latter by penalties and by absorbing all subjects of taxation; if a system leading to consolidation may be formed or pursued; and if, instead of leaving it to the respective states to encourage their agriculture or manufactures as their local interest may dictate, the general government may by bounties or protecting duties tax the one to promote the other; then the Constitution has not sufficiently provided for the continuance of the union by securing the rights of the state governments and local interests.

5. It is necessary for the preservation of republican government that the legislative, executive, and judiciary powers should be kept separate and distinct from each other, so that no man or body of men shall be authorized to exercise more than one of them at the same time. The Constitution, therefore, in consigning to the federal Senate a participation in the powers of each department, violates this important principle and tends to create in that body a dangerous aristocracy.

6. An essential principle of representative government is that it be influenced by the will of the people, which will can never be expressed if such representatives are corrupted or influenced by hopes of office. If this hope may multiply offices and extend patronage, if the president may nominate to valuable offices members of the legislature who shall please him and displease the people by increasing his power and patronage, if he may be tempted to use this power and patronage for securing his reelection, and if he may even bestow lucrative

diplomas upon judges whilst they are receiving liberal salaries paid as the price of their independence and purity, then a risk exists lest the legislature should legislate, the judges decide, and the senator concur in nominations with an eye to those offices, and lest the president may appoint with a view to his reelection; and thus may at length appear the phenomenon of a government republican in form without possessing a single chaste organ for expressing the public will.

Many of these observations were foreseen when the Constitution was ratified by those who voted for its adoption but waived then because of the vast importance of the union, which a rejection might have placed in hazard, of the provision made for amendments as trial should discover defects, and the hope that in the meantime the instrument, with all its defects, might produce social happiness if a proper tone was given to the government by the several agents in its operation. But since experience has evinced that much mischief may be done under an unwise administration, and that even the most valuable parts of the Constitution may be evaded or violated, we count no longer to rest our security upon the vain hope which depends on the rectitude of fallible men in successive administrations. But now that the union is as firmly established by the general opinion of the citizens as we can ever hope it to be, it behooves us to bring forward amendments which may fix it upon principles capable of restraining human passions.

Having, I trust, shown the utility and necessity of such efforts at this time, I will venture to submit to the consideration of my fellow citizens, with great humility and deference, whether it would not be advisable to have the Constitution amended:

1. By rendering a president ineligible for the next turn and transferring from him to the legislature the appointment of the judges and stationary foreign ministers, making the stipends of the latter to be no longer discretionary in the president.

"The Danger Not Over" from the Richmond *Examiner*, October 1801, by Edmund Pendleton (1801)

2. By depriving the senate of all executive power and shortening their term of service, or subjecting its members to removal by their constituents.

3. By rendering members of the legislature and the judges whilst in office {and} for a limited time thereafter incapable of taking any other office whatsoever (the offices of president and vice president excepted) and subjecting the judges to removal by the concurring vote of both houses of Congress.

4. By forming some check upon the abuse of public credit, which, though in some instances useful, like fleets and armies, may, like those, be carried to extremes dangerous to liberty and inconsistent with economical government.

5. By instituting a fair mode of impaneling juries.

6. By declaring that no treaty with a foreign nation, so far as it may relate to peace or war, to the expenditure of public money, or to commercial regulations, shall be law until ratified by the legislature, the interval between such treaty and the next meeting of Congress excepted, so far as it may not relate to the grant of money.

7. By defining prohibited powers so explicitly as to defy the wiles of construction. If nothing more should be gained, it will be a great acquisition clearly to interdict laws relating to the freedom of speech, of the press, and of religion, to declare that the common law of England or of any other foreign country in criminal cases shall not be considered as a law of the United States, and that treason shall be confined to the cases stated in the Constitution, so as not to be extended further by law or construction or by using other terms such as sedition, etc.

8. By marking out with more precision the distinct powers of the *general* and *state* governments.

In the Virginia Bill of Rights is expressed this inestimable sentiment:

> That no free government, or the blessing of liberty, can be preserved to any people but by a firm adherence to justice, moderation, temperance, frugality, and virtue, and by frequent recurrence to fundamental principles.

A sentiment produced, no doubt, by the experience of this melancholy truth, "That of men advanced to power, more are inclined to destroy liberty than to defend it; there is of course a continual effort for its destruction, which ought to be met by correspondent efforts for its preservation."

These principles and propositions are most respectfully submitted to my fellow citizens with this observation: that it is only when great and good men are at the head of a nation that the people can expect to succeed in forming such barriers to counteract recent encroachments on their rights; and whenever a nation is so supine as to suffer such an opportunity to be lost, they will soon feel that *the danger was not over*.

A Brief Inquiry into the True Nature and Character of Our Federal Government

By Abel P. Upshur

———— 1840 ————

Preface

The book to which the following pages relate has been for several years before the public. It has been reviewed in some of the principal periodicals of the country, and recommended in the strongest terms to public favor. I have no disposition to detract from its merits as a valuable compendium of historical facts, or as presenting just views of the Constitution in many respects. My attention has been directed to its political principles alone, and my sole purpose has been to inquire into the correctness of those principles, so far as they relate to the true nature and character of our Federal Government.

It may well excite surprise that so elaborate a work as this of Judge Story, and one so well calculated to influence public opinion, should have remained so long unnoticed by those who do not concur in the author's views. No one can regret this circumstance more than I do; for I would willingly have devolved upon abler hands the task which I now have undertaken. I offer no apology for the manner in which that task has been performed. It is enough for me to say, that the reader, howsoever unfavorable his opinion of this essay may be, will not be more sensible of its imperfections than I am. I know that the actual practice of the federal government for many years past, and the strong tendencies of public opinion in favor of federal power, forbid me to hope for a favorable reception, except from the very few who still cherish the principles which I have endeavored to re-establish.

The following essay was prepared about three years ago, with a view to its publication in one of our periodical reviews. Circumstances, which it is unnecessary to mention, prevented this from being done, and the work was laid aside and forgotten. My attention has been again called to it within a few weeks past, and I am now induced to give it to the public, under the hope that it may not be without its influence in directing the attention of those who have not yet lost all interest in the subject, to the true principles of our constitution of government.

I do not claim the merit of originality. My conclusions are drawn from the authentic information of history, and from a train of reasoning, which will occur to every mind, on the facts which history discloses. My object will be answered, if even the few by whom these pages will probably be read shall be induced to re-examine, with a sincere desire after truth, the great principles upon which political parties in our country were once divided, but which there is much reason to fear are no longer respected, even if they be not wholly forgotten.

I do not offer this essay as a commentary on the Federal Constitution. Having proposed to myself but a single object, I have endeavored to compress my matter within as small a compass as possible, consistent with a due degree to clearness, and a proper reference to authorities, where authorities are relied on.

A Brief Inquiry into the True Nature and Character of Our Federal Government
by Abel P. Upshur (1840)

THE

TRUE NATURE AND CHARACTER

OF OUR

FEDERAL GOVERNMENT:

A REVIEW

COMMENTARIES ON THE CONSTITUTION OF THE UNITED STATES, WITH A PRELIMINARY REVIEW OF THE CONSTITUTIONAL HISTORY OF THE COLONIES AND STATES BEFORE THE ADOPTION OF THE CONSTITUTION. BY JOSEPH STORY, LL.D., DANE PROFESSOR OF LAW IN HARVARD UNIVERSITY.

{Chapter I}

It came within the range of Judge Story's duties, as Dane Professor of Law in Harvard University, to expound and illustrate the Constitution of the United States. His lectures upon that subject have been abridged by himself, and published in a separate volume, under the above title. Although the work is given to the public as an abridgment, it is nevertheless, as it professes to be, "a full analysis and exposition of the constitution of government of the United States"; and presents, in the opinion of the author himself, the "leading doctrines" of the original, "so far as they are necessary to a just understanding of the actual provisions of the Constitution." The author professes to have compiled it "for the use of colleges and high schools"; but as it contains all the important historical facts, and all the leading reasons upon which his own opinions have been based, and as it has been prepared with elaborate care in other respects, we may reasonably suppose, without impeaching his modesty, that he expected it to be received as a complete work. It is, indeed, quite as full as any such work needs to be, for any purpose, except, perhaps, the very first lessons to the student of constitutional law. The politician and the jurist may consult it, with a certainty of finding all the prominent topics of the subject fully discussed.

A work presenting a proper analysis and correct views of the Constitution of the United States has long been a desideratum with the public. It is true that the last fifteen years have not been unfruitful in commentaries upon that instrument; *such* commentaries, however, as have, for the most part, met a deserved fate, in immediate and total oblivion. Most of them have served only to throw ridicule upon the subject which they professed to illustrate. A few have appeared, however, of a much higher order, and bearing the stamp of talent, learning, and research. Among these, the work before us and the Commentaries of Chief Justice Kent, hold the first rank. Both of these works are, as it is natural they should be, strongly tinctured with the political opinions of their respective authors; and as there is a perfect concurrence between them in this respect, their joint authority can scarcely fail to exert a strong influence upon public opinion. It is much to be regretted that someone, among the many who differ from them in their views of the Constitution, and who possess all the requisite qualifications for the task, should not have thought it necessary to vindicate his own peculiar tenets, in a work equally elaborate, and presenting just claims to public attention. The authority of great names is of such imposing weight, that mere reason and argument can rarely counterpoise it in the public mind; and its preponderance is not easily overcome, except by adding like authority to the weight of reason and argument, in the opposing scale. I hope it is not yet too late for this suggestion to have its effect upon those to whom it is addressed.

The first commentary upon the Constitution, the Federalist, is decidedly the best which has yet appeared. The writers of that book were actors in all the interesting scenes of the period, and two of them were members of the convention which formed the Constitution. Added to this, their extensive information, their commanding talents, and their experience in great public affairs, qualified them, in a peculiar degree, for the task which they undertook. Nevertheless, their great object was to *recommend* the Constitution to the people, at a time when it was very uncertain whether they would adopt it or not; and hence their work, although it contains a very full and philosophical analysis of the subject, comes to us as a mere argument in support of a favorite measure, and, for that reason, does not always command our entire confidence. Besides, the Constitution was then untried, and its true character, which is to be learned only from its practical operation, could only be conjectured. Much has been developed, in the actual practice of the government, which no politician of that day could either have foreseen or imagined. New questions have arisen, not then anticipated, and difficulties and embarrassments, wholly unforeseen, have sprung from new events in the relation of the States to one another, and to the general government. Hence the Federalist cannot be relied on, as full and safe authority in all cases. It is, indeed, matter of just surprise, and affording the strongest proof of the profound wisdom and far-seeing sagacity of the authors of that work, that their views of the Constitution have been so often justified in the course of its practical operation. Still, however, it must be admitted that the Federalist is defective in some important particulars, and deficient in many more. The Constitution is much better understood at this day than at the time of its adoption. This is not true of the great principles of civil and political liberty, which lie at the foundation of that instrument; but it is emphatically true of some of its provisions, which were considered at the time as comparatively unimportant, or so plain as not to be misunderstood, but which have been shown, by subsequent events, to be pregnant with the greatest difficulties, and to exert the most important influence upon the whole character of the government. Contemporary expositions of the Constitution, therefore, although they should be received as authority in *some* cases, and may enlighten our judgments in most others, cannot be regarded as safe guides, by the expounder of that instrument at this day. The subject demands our attention now as strongly as it did before the Federalist was written.

It is not surprising, therefore, that the work now under consideration should have been hailed with pleasure, and received with every favorable disposition. Judge Story fills a high station in the judiciary of the United States, and has acquired a character, for talents and learning, which ensures respect to whatever he may publish under his own name. His duty, as a judge of the supreme court, has demanded of him frequent investigations of the nicest questions of constitutional law; and his long service in that capacity has probably brought under his review every provision of that instrument, in regard to which any difference of opinion has prevailed. Assisted as he has been by the arguments of the ablest counsel, and by the joint deliberations of the other judges of the court, it would be indeed wonderful, if he should hazard his well-earned reputation as a jurist, upon any hasty or unweighted opinion, upon subjects so grave and important. He has also been an attentive observer of political events, and although by no means obtrusive in politics, has yet a political character, scarcely less distinguished than his character as a jurist. To all these claims to public attention and respect, may be added a reputation for laborious research, and for calm and temperate thinking. A work on the Constitution of the United States, emanating from such a source, cannot fail to exert a strong influence upon public opinion, and it is, therefore, peculiarly important that its real character should be understood. Whatever may be the cast of its political opinions, it can scarcely fail to contain many valuable truths, and much information which will be found useful to all classes of readers. And, so far as its political opinions are concerned, it is of the highest importance to guard the public mind against the influence which its errors, if errors they be, may borrow from the mere authority of the distinguished name under which they are advanced.

The plan of the work before us is very judicious. In order to a correct understanding of the Constitution, it is absolutely necessary to understand the situation of the States before it was adopted. The author, acting upon this idea, distributes his work into three great divisions. "The first will embrace a sketch of the charters, constitutional history, and ante-revolutionary jurisprudence of the colonies. The second will embrace the constitutional history of the States, during the revolution, and the rise, progress, decline, and fall of the confederation. The third will embrace the history of the rise and adoption of the Constitution, and a full exposition of all its provisions, with the reasons on which they were respectively founded, the objections by which they were respectively assailed, and such illustrations drawn from contemporaneous documents, and the subsequent operations of the government, as may best enable the reader to estimate for himself, the true value of each." This plan is at once comprehensive and analytic. It embraces every topic necessary to a full understanding of the subject, while, at the same time, it presents them in the natural order of investigation. It displays a perfect acquaintance with the true nature of the subject, and promises every result which the reader can desire. The first part relates to a subject of the greatest interest to every American, and well worthy the study of philosophical inquirers, all over the world. There is not, within the whole range of history, an event more important, with reference to its effects upon the world at large, than the settlement of the American colonies. It did not fall within the plan of our author to inquire very extensively, or very minutely, into the mere history of events which distinguished that extraordinary enterprise. So far as the first settlers may be regarded as actuated by avarice, by ambition, or by any other of the usual motives of the adventurer, their deeds belong to the province of the historian alone. We, however, must contemplate them in another and a higher character. A deep and solemn feeling of religion, and an attachment to, and an understanding of, the principles of civil liberty, far in advance of the age in which they lived, suggested to most of them the idea of seeking a new home, and founding new institutions in the western world. To this spirit we are indebted for all that is free and liberal in our present political systems. It would be a work of very great interest, and altogether worthy of the political historian to trace the great principles of our institutions back to their sources. Their origin would probably be discovered at a period much more remote than is generally supposed. We should derive from such a review much light in the interpretation of those parts of our systems, as to which we have no precise rules in the language of our constitutions of government. It is to be regretted that Judge Story did not take this view of the subject. Although not strictly required by the plan of his work, it was, nevertheless, altogether consistent with it, and would have added much to its interest with the general reader. His sources of historical information were ample, and his habits and the character of his mind fitted him well for such an investigation, and for presenting the result in an analytic and philosophical form. He has chosen, however, to confine himself within much narrower limits. Yet, even within those limits, he has brought together a variety of historical facts of great interest, and has presented them in a condensed form, well calculated to make a lasting impression upon the memory. The brief sketch which he has given of the settlement of the several colonies, and of the charters from which they derived their rights and powers as separate governments, contains much to enable us to understand fully the relation which they bore to one another and to the mother country. This is the true starting point in the investigation of those vexed questions of constitutional law which have so long divided political parties in the United States. It would seem almost impossible that any two opinions could exist upon the subject; and yet the historical facts, upon which alone all parties must rely, although well authenticated and comparatively recent, have not been understood by all men alike. Our author was well aware of the importance of settling this question at the threshold of his work. Many of the powers which have been claimed for the federal government, by the political party to which he belongs, depend upon a denial of that separate existence, and separate sovereignty and independence, which the opposing party has uniformly claimed for the States. It is, therefore, highly important to the correct settlement of this controversy, that we should ascertain the precise political condition of the several colonies prior to the revolution. This will enable us to determine how far our author has done justice to his subject, in the execution of the first part of his plan; and by tracing the colonies from their first establishment as such, through the various stages of their progress up to the adoption of the Federal Constitution, we shall be greatly aided in forming a correct opinion as to the true character of that instrument.

{Chapter II}

It appears to be a favorite object with the author to impress upon the mind of the reader, at the very commencement of his work, the idea that the people of the several colonies were, as to some objects, which he has not explained, and to some extent, which he has not defined, "one people." This is not only plainly inferable from the general scope of the book, but is expressly asserted in the following passage: "But although the colonies were independent of each other in respect to their domestic concerns, they were not wholly alien to each other. On the contrary, they were fellow-subjects, and for many purposes one people. Every colonist had a right to inhabit, if he pleased, in any other colony, and as a British subject he was capable of inheriting lands by descent in every other colony. The commercial intercourse of the colonies too was regulated by the general laws of the British empire, and could not be restrained or obstructed by colonial legislation. The remarks of Mr. Chief Justice Jay are equally just and striking: 'All the people of this country were then subjects of the king of Great Britain, and owed allegiance to him, and all the civil authority then existing or exercised here flowed from the head of the British empire. They were in a strict sense *fellow-subjects* and in a variety of respects *one people*. When the revolution commenced, the patriots did not assert that only the same affinity and social connection subsisted between the people of the colonies, which subsisted between the people of Gaul, Britain, and Spain, while Roman provinces, to wit, only that affinity and social connection which results from the mere circumstance of being governed by the same prince.'"

In this passage the author takes his ground distinctly and boldly. The first idea suggested by the perusal of it is, that he discerned very clearly the necessity of establishing his position, but did not discern quite so clearly by what process of reasoning he was to accomplish it. If the passage stood alone, it would be fair to suppose that he did not design to extend the idea of a unity among the people of the colonies beyond the several particulars which he has enumerated.

Justice to him requires that we should suppose this; for, if it had been otherwise, he would scarcely have failed to support his opinion by pointing out some one of the "many purposes," for which the colonies were, in his view of them, "one people." The same may be said of Mr. Chief Justice Jay. He also has specified several particulars in which he supposed this unity to exist, and arrives at the conclusion, that the people of the several colonies were, "in a variety of respects, one people." In what respect they were "one," except those which he has enumerated, he does not say, and of course it is fair to presume that he meant to rest the justness of his conclusion upon them alone. The historical facts stated by both of these gentlemen are truly stated; but it is surprising that it did not occur to such cool reasoners, that every one of them is *the result of the relation between the colonies and the mother country, and not the result of the relation between the colonies themselves*. Every British subject, whether born in England proper or in a colony, has a right to reside anywhere within the British realm; and this *by the force of British laws*. Such is the right of every Englishman, wherever he may be found. As to the right of the colonist to inherit lands by descent in any other colony than his own, our author himself informs us that it belonged to him "as a British subject." That right, indeed, is in consequence of his allegiance. By the policy of the British constitution and laws, it is not permitted that the soil of her territory should belong to any from whom she cannot demand all the duties of allegiance. This allegiance is the same in all the colonies as it is in England proper; and, wherever it exists, the correspondent right to own and inherit the soil attaches. The right to regulate commercial intercourse among her colonies belongs, of course, to the parent country, unless she relinquishes it by some act of her own; and no such act is shown in the present case. On the contrary, although that right was resisted for a time by some of the American colonies, it was finally yielded, as our author himself informs us, by all those of New England, and I am not informed that it was denied by any other. Indeed, the supremacy of parliament, in most matters of legislation which concerned the colonies, was generally – nay, *universally* – admitted, up to the very eve of the revolution. It is true, the right to *tax* the colonies was denied, but this was upon a wholly different principle. It was the right of every British subject to be exempt from taxation, except by his own consent; and as the colonies were not, and from their local situation could not be, represented in parliament, the right of that body to tax them was denied, upon a fundamental principle of English liberty. But the right of the mother country to regulate commerce among her colonies is of a different character, and it never was denied to England by her American colonies, so long as a hope of reconciliation remained to them. In like manner, the facts relied on by Mr. Jay, that "all people of this country were then subjects of the king of Great Britain, and owed allegiance to him," and that "all the civil authority then existing or exercised here flowed from the head of the British empire," are but the usual incidents of colonial dependence, and are by no means peculiar to the case he was considering. They do, indeed, prove a unity between all the colonies and *the mother country*, and show that these, taken altogether, are, in the strictest sense of the terms, "one people"; but I am at a loss to perceive how they prove, that two or more parts or subdivisions of the same empire necessarily constitute "one people." If this be true of the colonies, it is equally true of any two or more geographical sections of England proper; for every one of the reasons assigned applies as strictly to this case as to that of the colonies. Any two countries may be "one people," or "a nation de facto," if they can be made so by the facts that their people are "subjects of the king of Great Britain, and owe allegiance to him," and that "all the civil authority exercised therein flows from the head of the British empire."

It is to be regretted that the author has not given us his own views of the sources from which these several rights and powers were derived. If they authorize his conclusion, that there was any sort of unity among the people of the several colonies, distinct from their common connection with the mother country, as parts of the same empire, it must be because they flowed from something in the relation betwixt the colonies themselves, and not from their common relation to the parent country. Nor is it enough that these rights and powers should, *in point of fact*, flow from the relation of the colonies to one another; they must be the *necessary result of their political condition*. Even admitting, then, that they would, under any state of circumstances, warrant the conclusion which the author has drawn from them, it does not follow that the conclusion is correctly drawn in the present instance. For aught that he has said to the contrary, the right of every colonist to inhabit and inherit lands in every colony, whether his own or not, may have been derived from positive compact and agreement among the colonies themselves; and this presupposes that they were distinct and separate, and not "one people." And so far as the rights of the mother country are concerned, they existed in the same form, and to the same extent, over every other colony of the empire. Did this make the people of *all* the colonies "one people"? If so, the people of Jamaica, the British East India possessions, and the Canadas are, for the very same reason, "one people" at this day. If a common allegiance to a common sovereign, and a common subordination to his jurisdiction, are sufficient to make the people of different countries "one people," it is not perceived (with all deference to Mr. Chief Justice Jay) why the people of Gaul, Britain, and Spain might not have been "one people," while Roman provinces, notwithstanding "the patriots" did not say so. The *general* relation between the colonies and the parent country is as well settled and understood as any other, and it is precisely the same in all cases, except where special consent and agreement may vary it. Whoever, therefore, would prove that any peculiar *unity* existed between the American colonies, is bound to show something in their charters, or some peculiarity in their condition, to exempt them from the general rule. Judge Story was too well acquainted with the state of the facts to make any such attempt in the present case. The congress of the nine colonies, which assembled at New York, in October, 1765, declare that the colonists "owe the same allegiance to the crown of Great Britain, that is owing from his subjects born within the realm, and all due subordination to that august body, the parliament of Great Britain." "That the colonists are entitled to all the inherent rights and liberties of his [the king's] natural born subjects within the kingdom of Great Britain." We have here an all-sufficient foundation of the right of the crown to regulate commerce among the colonies, and of the right of the colonists to inhabit and to inherit land in each and all the colonies. They were nothing more than the ordinary rights and liabilities of every British subject; and, indeed, the most that the colonies ever contended for was an equality, in these respects, with the subjects born in England. The facts, therefore, upon which our author's reasoning is founded, spring from a different source from that from which he is compelled to derive them, in order to support his conclusion.

So far as the author's argument is concerned, the subject might be permitted to rest here. Indeed, one would be tempted to think, from the apparent carelessness and indifference with which the argument is urged, that he himself did not attach to it any particular importance. It is not his habit to dismiss grave matters with such slight examination, nor does it consist with the character of his mind to be satisfied with reasoning which bears even a doubtful relation to his subject. Neither can it be supposed that he would be willing to rely on the simple *ipse dixit* of Chief Justice Jay, unsupported by argument, unsustained by any references to historical facts, and wholly indefinite in extent and bearing. Why, then, was this passage written? As mere history, apart from its bearing on the Constitution of the United States, it is of no value in this work, and is wholly out of place. All doubts upon this subject will be removed in the progress of this examination. The great effort of the author, throughout the entire work, is to establish the doctrine, that the Constitution of the United States is a government of "the people of the United States," as contradistinguished from the people of the several States; or, in other words, that it is a consolidated, and not a federative system. His construction of every contested federal power depends mainly upon this distinction; and hence the necessity of establishing a *one-ness* among the people of the several colonies, prior to the revolution. It may well excite our surprise, that a proposition so necessary to the principal design of the work, should be stated with so little precision, and dismissed with so little effort to sustain it by argument. One so well informed as Judge Story, of the state of political opinions in this country, could scarcely have supposed that it would be received as an admitted truth, requiring no examination. It enters too deeply into grave questions of constitutional law, to be so summarily disposed of. We should not be content, therefore, with simply proving that the author has assigned no sufficient reason for the opinion he has advanced. The subject demands of us the still farther proof that his opinion is, in fact, erroneous, and that it cannot be sustained by any *other* reasons.

In order to constitute "one people," in a political sense, of the inhabitants of different countries, something more is necessary than that they should owe a common allegiance to a common sovereign. Neither is it sufficient that, in some particulars, they are bound alike, by laws which that sovereign may prescribe; nor does the question depend on geographical relations. The inhabitants of different islands may be one people, and those of contiguous countries may be, as we know they in fact are, different nations. By the term "people," as here used, we do not mean merely a number of persons. We mean by it a political corporation, the members of which owe a common allegiance to a common sovereignty, and do not owe any allegiance which is *not* common; who are bound by no laws except such as that sovereignty may prescribe; who owe to one another reciprocal obligations; who possess common political interests; who are liable to common political duties; and who can exert no sovereign power except in the name of the whole. Anything short of this, would be an imperfect definition of that political corporation which we call a "people."

Tested by this definition, the people of the American colonies were, in no conceivable sense, "one people." They owed, indeed, allegiance to the British king, as the head of each colonial government, and as forming a part thereof; but this allegiance was exclusive, in each colony, to its own government, and, consequently, to the king as the head thereof, and was not a common allegiance of the people of all the colonies, to a common head.* These colonial governments were clothed with the sovereign power of making laws, and of enforcing obedience to them, from their own people. The people of one colony owed no allegiance to the government of any other colony, and were not bound by its laws. The colonies had no common legislature, no common treasury, no common military power, no common judicatory. The people of one colony were not liable to pay taxes to any other colony, nor to bear arms in its defense; they had no right to vote in its elections; no influence nor control in its municipal government, no interest in its municipal institutions. There was no prescribed form by which the colonies could act together, for any purpose whatever; they were not known as "one people" in any one function of government. Although they were all, alike, dependencies of the British crown, yet, even in the action of the parent country, in regard to them, they were recognized as separate and distinct. They were established at different times, and each under an authority from the crown, which applied to itself alone. They were not even alike in their organization. Some were provincial, some proprietary, and some charter governments. Each derived its form of government from the particular instrument establishing it, or from assumptions of power acquiesced in by the crown, without any connection with, or relation to, any other. They stood upon the same footing, in every respect, with other British colonies, with nothing to distinguish their relation either to the parent country or to one another. The charter of any one of them might have been destroyed, without in any manner affecting the rest. In point of fact, the charters of nearly all of them were altered, from time to time, and the whole character of their governments changed. These changes were made in each colony for itself alone, sometimes by its own action, sometimes by the power and authority of the crown; but never by the joint agency of any other colony, and never with reference to the wishes or demands of any other colony. Thus they were separate and distinct in their creation;

---

* The resolutions of Virginia, in 1765, show that she considered herself merely as an appendage of the British crown; that *her* legislature was alone authorized to tax her; and that she had a right to call on *her* king, who was also king of England, to protect her against the usurpations of the British parliament.

separate and distinct in the forms of their governments; separate and distinct in the changes and modifications of their governments, which were made from time to time; separate and distinct in political functions, in political rights, and in political duties.

The provincial government of Virginia was the first established. The people of Virginia owed allegiance to the British king, as the head of their own local government. The authority of that government was confined within certain geographical limits, known as Virginia, and all who lived within those limits were "one people." When the colony of Plymouth was subsequently settled, were the people of that colony "one" with the people of Virginia? When, long afterwards, the proprietary government of Pennsylvania was established, were the followers of William Penn "one" with the people of Plymouth and Virginia? If so, to which government was their allegiance due? Virginia had a government of her own, Pennsylvania a government of her own, and Massachusetts a government of her own. The people of Pennsylvania could not be equally bound by the laws of all three governments, because those laws might happen to conflict; they could not owe the duties of citizenship to all of them alike, because they *might* stand in hostile relations to one another. Either, then, the government of Virginia, which originally extended over the whole territory, continued to be supreme therein, (subject only to its dependence upon the British crown), or else its supremacy was yielded to the new government. Everyone knows that this last was the case; that within the territory of the new government the authority of that government alone prevailed. How then could the people of this new government of Pennsylvania be said to be "one" with the people of Virginia, when they were not citizens of Virginia, owed her no allegiance and no duty, and when their allegiance to another government might place them in the relation of enemies of Virginia?

In farther illustration of this point, let us suppose that some one of the colonies had refused to unite in the declaration of independence; what relation would it then have held to the others? Not having disclaimed its allegiance to the British crown, it would still have continued to be a British colony, subject to the authority of the parent country, in all respects as before. Could the other colonies have rightfully compelled it to unite with them in their revolutionary purposes, on the ground that it was part and parcel of the "one people," known as the people of the colonies? No such right was ever claimed, or dreamed of, and it will scarcely be contended for now, in the face of the known history of the time. Such recusant colony would have stood precisely as did the Canadas, and every other part of the British empire. The colonies, which had declared war, would have considered its people as enemies, but would not have had a right to treat them as traitors, or as disobedient citizens resisting their authority. To what purpose, then, were the people of the colonies "one people," if, in a case so important to the common welfare, there was no right in all the people together, to coerce the members of their own community to the performance of a common duty?

It is thus apparent that the people of the colonies were not "one people," as to any purpose involving allegiance on the one hand, or protection on the other. What then, I again ask, are the "many purposes" to which the author alludes? It is certainly incumbent on him who asserts this identity, against the inferences most naturally deducible from the historical facts, to show at what time, by what process, and for what purposes, it was affected. He claims too much consideration for his personal authority, when he requires his readers to reject the plain information of history, in favor of his bare assertion. The charters of the colonies prove no identity between them, but the reverse; and it has already been shown that this identity is not the necessary result of their common relation to the mother country. By what other means they came to be "one," in any intelligible and political sense, it remains for the author to explain.

If these views of the subject be not convincing, the author himself has furnished proof, in all needful abundance, of the incorrectness of his own conclusion. He tells us that, "though the colonies had a common origin, and owed a common allegiance, and the inhabitants of each were British subjects, *they had no direct political connection with each other.* Each was independent of all the others; each, in a limited sense, was sovereign within its own territory. There was neither alliance nor confederacy between them. The assembly of one province could not make laws for another, nor confer privileges which were to be enjoyed or exercised in another, farther than they could be in any independent foreign state. As colonies they were also excluded from all connection with foreign states. They were known only as dependencies, and they followed the fate of the parent country, both in peace and war, without having assigned to them, in the intercourse or diplomacy of nations, any distinct or independent existence. *They did not possess the power of forming any league or treaty among themselves, which would acquire an obligatory force, without the assent of the parent State.* And though their mutual wants and necessities often induced them to associate for common purposes of defense, these confederacies were of a casual and temporary nature, and were allowed as an indulgence, rather than as a right. They made several efforts to procure the establishment of some general superintending government over them all; but their own differences of opinion, as well as the jealousy of the crown, made these efforts abortive."

The English language affords no terms stronger than those which are here used to convey the idea of separateness, distinctness and independence, among the colonies. No commentary could make the description plainer, or more full and complete. The *unity*, contended for by the author, nowhere appears, but is distinctly disaffirmed in every sentence. The colonies were not only distinct in their creation, and in the powers and faculties of their governments, but there was not even "an alliance or confederacy between them." They had "no general superintending government over them all," and tried in vain to establish one. Each was "independent of all the others," having its own legislature, and without power to confer either right or privilege beyond its own territory. "Each, in a limited sense, was sovereign within its own territory"; and to sum up all, in a single sentence, "they had no direct political connection with each other!" The condition of the colonies was, indeed, anomalous, if our author's view of it be correct. They presented the singular spectacle of "one people," or political corporation, the members of which had "no direct political connection with each other," and who had not the power to form such connection, even "by league or treaty among themselves."

This brief review will, it is believed, be sufficient to convince the reader that our author has greatly mistaken the real condition and relation of the colonies, in supposing that they formed "one people," in any sense, or for any purpose whatever. He is entitled to credit, however, for the candor with which he has stated the historical facts. Apart from all other sources of information, his book affords to every reader abundant materials for the formation of his own opinion, and for enabling him to decide satisfactorily whether the author's inferences from the facts, which he himself has stated, be warranted by them, or not.

{Chapter III}

In the execution of the second division of his plan, very little was required of the author, either as a historian or a commentator. Accordingly, he has alluded but slightly to the condition of the colonies during the existence of the revolutionary government, and has sketched with great rapidity, yet sufficiently in detail, the rise, decline and fall of the Confederation. Even here, however, he has fallen into some errors, and has ventured to express decisive and important opinions, without due warrant. The desire to make "the people of the United States" one consolidated nation is so strong and predominant, that it breaks forth, often uncalled for, in every part of his work. He tells us that the first congress of the Revolution was "a general or national government"; that it "was organized under the auspices and with the consent of *the people*, acting directly in their primary, sovereign capacity, and without the intervention of the functionaries to whom the ordinary powers of government were delegated in the colonies." He acknowledges that the powers of this congress were but ill-defined; that many of them were exercised by mere usurpation, and were acquiesced in by the people, only from the confidence reposed in the wisdom and patriotism of its members, and because there was no proper opportunity, during the pressure of the war, to raise nice questions of the powers of government. And yet he infers, from the exercise of powers thus ill-defined, and, in great part, usurped, that "from the moment of the declaration of independence, if not for most purposes at an antecedent period, the united colonies must be considered as being a nation *de facto*," &c.

A very slight attention to the history of the times will place this subject in its true light. The colonies complained of oppressions from the mother country, and were anxious to devise some means by which their grievances might be redressed. These grievances were common to all of them; for England made no discrimination between them, in the general course of her colonial policy. Their rights, as British subjects, had never been well defined; and some of the most important of these rights, as asserted by themselves, had been denied by the British crown. As early as 1765 a majority of the colonies had met together in congress, or convention, in New York, for the purpose of deliberating on these grave matters of common concern; and they then made a formal declaration of what they considered their rights, as colonists and British subjects. This measure, however, led to no redress of their grievances. On the contrary, the subsequent measures of the British government gave new and just causes of complaint; so that, in 1774, it was deemed necessary that the colonies should again meet together, in order to consult upon their general condition, and provide for the safety of their common rights. Hence the congress which met at Carpenters' Hall, in Philadelphia, on the 5th of September, 1774. It consisted of delegates from New Hampshire, Massachusetts Bay, Rhode Island and Providence Plantations, Connecticut, *from the city and county of New York, and other counties in the province of New York*, New Jersey, Pennsylvania, *Newcastle, Kent, and Sussex in Delaware*, Maryland, Virginia, and South Carolina. North Carolina was not represented until the 14th September, and Georgia not at all. It is also apparent, that New York was not represented *as a colony*, but only through certain portions of her people;* in like manner, Lyman Hall was admitted to his seat, in the succeeding congress, as a delegate from the parish of St. Johns, in Georgia, although he declined to vote on

---

* The historical fact here stated, is perfectly authenticated, and has never been disputed; nevertheless, the following extracts from the Journals of Congress, may not be out of place.

"Wednesday, September 14, 1774. Henry Wisner, a delegate from *the county of Orange*, in the colony of New York, appeared at congress, and produced a certificate of his election *by the said county*, which being read and approved, he took his seat in congress as a deputy from the colony of New York."

"Monday, September 26, 1774. John Hening, Esq., a deputy from *Orange county*, in the colony of New York, appeared this morning, and took his seat as a deputy from that colony."

"Saturday, October 1, 1774. Simon Bocrum, Esq., appeared in congress as a deputy from King's county, in the colony of New York, and produced the credentials of his election, which being read and approved, he took his seat as a delegate from that colony."

It is evident from these extracts, that although the delegates from certain portions of the people of New York were admitted to seats in congress as delegates *from the colony*, yet, in point of fact, they were not *elected* as such, neither were they ever recognized as such, by New York herself. The truth is, as will presently appear, the majority of her people were not ripe for the measures pursued by congress, and would not have agreed to appoint delegates for the whole colony.

any question requiring a majority of *the colonies* to carry it, because he was not the representative of a colony. This congress passed a variety of important resolutions, between September, 1774, and the 22nd October, in the same year; during all which time Georgia was not represented at all; for even the parish of St. John's did not appoint a representative till May, 1775. In point of fact, the congress was *a deliberative and advisory* body, and nothing more; and, for this reason, it was not deemed important, or, at least, not *indispensable*, that all the colonies should be represented, since the resolutions of congress had no obligatory force whatever. It was appointed for the sole purpose of taking into consideration the general condition of the colonies, and of devising and recommending proper measures, for the security of their rights and interests. For these objects no precise powers and instructions were necessary, and *beyond* them none were given. Neither does it appear that any precise time was assigned for the duration of congress. The duty with which it was charged was extremely simple; and it was taken for granted that it would dissolve itself as soon as the duty should be performed.*

---

* A reference to the credentials of the congress of 1774 will show, beyond all doubt, the true character of that assembly. The following are extracts from them.

New Hampshire. "To *devise, consult and adopt* such measures as may have the most likely tendency to extricate the colonies from their present difficulties; to secure and perpetuate their rights, liberties and privileges, and to restore that peace, harmony and mutual confidence, which once happily subsisted between the parent country and her colonies."

Massachusetts. "To *consult* on the present state of the colonies, and the miseries to which they are, and must be reduced, by the operation of certain acts of parliament respecting America; and to deliberate and determine upon wise and proper measures *to be by them recommended to all the colonies*, for the recovery and establishment of their just rights and liberties, civil and religious, and the restoration of union and harmony between Great Britain and the colonies, most ardently desired by all good men."

Rhode Island. "To consult on proper measures to obtain a repeal of the several acts of the British parliament for levying taxes on his majesty's subjects in America without their consent, and upon proper measures to establish the rights and liberties of the colonies upon a just and solid foundation, *agreeably to instructions given by the general assembly*."

Connecticut. "To *consult and advise* on proper measures for advancing the best good of the colonies, and such conferences to report from time to time to the colonial house of representatives."

New York. Only a few of her counties were represented, some by deputies authorized to "represent," and some by deputies authorized to "attend congress."

It is perfectly apparent that the mere *appointment* of this congress

New Jersey. "To represent the colony in the general congress."

Pennsylvania. "To form and adopt a plan for the purposes of obtaining redress of American grievances, ascertaining American rights upon the most solid and constitutional principles, and for establishing that union and harmony between Great Britain and the colonies which is indispensably necessary to the welfare and happiness of both."

Delaware. "To consult and advise with the deputies from the other colonies, to determine upon all such prudent and lawful measures as may be judged most expedient for the colonies immediately and unitedly to adopt, in order to obtain relief for an oppressed people,[a] and the redress of our general grievances."

Maryland. "To attend a general congress, to effect one general plan of conduct operating on the commercial connection of the colonies with the mother country, for the relief of Boston and the preservation of American liberty."

Virginia. "To consider of the most proper and effectual manner of so operating on the commercial connection of the colonies with the mother country, as to procure redress for the much injured province of Massachusetts Bay, to secure British America from the ravage and ruin of arbitrary taxes, and speedily to procure the return of that harmony and union, so beneficial to the whole empire, and so ardently desired by all British America."

North Carolina. "To take such measures as they may deem prudent to effect the purpose of describing with certainty the rights of Americans, repairing the breach made in those rights, and for guarding them for the future from any such violations done under the sanction of public authority." For these purposes the delegates are "invested with such powers as may make any acts done by them *obligatory in honor*, on every inhabitant hereof, who is not an alien to his country's good, and an apostate to the liberties of America."

South Carolina. "To consider the acts lately passed, and bills depending in parliament with regard to the port of Boston, and Colony of Massachusetts Bay; which acts and bills, in the precedent and consequences, affect the whole continent of America. Also the grievances under which America labors, by reason of the several acts of parliament that impose taxes or duties for raising a revenue, and lay unnecessary restraints and burdens on trade; and of the statutes, parliamentary acts and royal instructions, which make an invidious distinction between his majesty's subjects in Great Britain and America, with full power and authority to concert, agree to and prosecute such legal measures, as in the opinion of the said deputies, so to be assembled, shall be most likely to obtain a repeal of the said acts, and a redress of those grievances."

[The above extracts are made from the credentials of the deputies of the several colonies, as spread upon the journal of congress, according to a copy of that journal bound (as appears by a gilt label on the back thereof) for the use of the president of congress — now in possession of B. Tucker, Esq.]

It is perfectly clear from these extracts, 1. That the colonies did not consider themselves as "one people," and that they were therefore bound to consider the quarrel of Boston as their own; but that they made common cause with Massachusetts, only because the *principles* asserted in regard to her, equally affected the other colonies; 2. That each colony appointed its own delegates, giving them precisely such power and authority as suited its own views; 3. That no colony gave any power or authority, except for advisement only; 4. That so far from designing to establish "a general or national government," and did not make the people of all the colonies "one people," nor a "nation *de facto*." All the colonies did not unite in the appointment, neither as colonies nor by any portion of their people acting in their primary assemblies, as has already been shown. The colonies were not independent, and had not even resolved to declare themselves so at any future time. On the contrary, they were extremely desirous to preserve and continue their connection with the parent country, and congress was charged with the duty of devising such measures as would enable them to do so, without involving a surrender of their rights as British subjects. It is equally clear that the powers, with which congress was clothed, did not flow from, nor *constitute* "one people," or "nation *de facto*," and that that body was not "a general or national government," nor a government of any kind whatever. The existence of such government was absolutely inconsistent with the allegiance which the colonies still acknowledged to the British crown. Our author himself informs us in a passage already quoted, that they had no power to form such government, nor to enter into "any league or treaty among themselves." Indeed, congress did not claim any legislative power whatever, nor could it have done so, consistently with the political relations which the colonies still acknowledged and desired to preserve. Its acts were in the form of *resolutions*, and not in the form of *laws*; it *recommended* to its constituents whatever it believed to be for their advantage, but it

---

[a] Massachusetts, the particular wrongs of which are just before recited at large.

to form themselves into "a nation *de facto*," their great purpose was to bring about a reconciliation and harmony with the mother country. This is still farther apparent from the tone of the public addresses of congress; 5. That this congress was not "organized under the auspices and with the consent of the people, acting directly in their primary, sovereign capacity, and without the intervention of the functionaries to whom the ordinary powers of government were delegated in the colonies," but, on the contrary, that it was organized by the colonies *as such*, and generally through their ordinary legislatures; and *always* with careful regard to their separate and independent rights and powers.

If the congress of 1774 was "a general or national government," neither New York nor Georgia was a party to it; for neither of them was represented in that congress. It is also worthy of remark that the congress of 1774 had no agents of its own in foreign countries, but employed those of the several colonies. See the resolution for delivering the address to the king, passed October 25, 1774, and the letter to the agents, approved on the following day.

commanded nothing. Each colony, and the people thereof, were at perfect liberty to act upon such recommendation or not, as they might think proper.*

On the 22nd October, 1774, this congress dissolved itself, having recommended to the several colonies to appoint delegates to another congress, to be held in Philadelphia in the following May. Accordingly delegates were chosen, as they had been chosen to the preceding congress, each colony and the people thereof acting for themselves, and by themselves; and the delegates thus chosen were clothed with substantially the same powers, for precisely the same objects, as in the former congress. Indeed, it could not have been otherwise; for the relations of the colonies were still unchanged, and any measure establishing "a general or national government," or uniting the colonies so as to constitute them "a nation *de facto*,"

---

* The journals of congress afford the most abundant and conclusive proofs of this. In order to show the general character of their proceedings it is enough for me to refer to the following:

On the 11th October, 1774, it was "Resolved unanimously, That a memorial be prepared to the people of British America, stating to them the necessity of a firm, united and invariable observation of the measures *recommended* by the congress, as they tender the invaluable rights and liberties derived to them from the laws and constitution of their country." The memorial was accordingly prepared, in conformity with the resolution.

Congress having previously had under consideration the plan of an association for establishing non-importation, &c., finally adopted it, October 20, 1774. After reciting their grievances, they say, "And, therefore, we do, for ourselves and the inhabitants of the several colonies whom we represent, firmly agree and associate, *under the sacred ties of virtue, honor and love of our country*, as follows." They then proceed to recommend a certain course of proceeding, such as non-importation and non-consumption of certain British productions, they recommended the appointment of a committee in every county, city and town, to watch their fellow citizens, in order to ascertain whether or not "any person within the limits of their appointment has violated this association," and if they should find any such, it is their duty to report them, "to the end, that all such foes to the rights of British America may be publicly known, and *universally contemned as the enemies of American liberty; and, thenceforth, we respectively will break off all dealings with him or her*." They also resolve, that they will "have no trade, commerce, dealings or intercourse whatsoever, with any colony or province in North America, which shall not accede to, or which shall hereafter violate, this association, but will hold them as unworthy of the rights of freemen, and as inimical to the liberties of their country."

This looks very little like the legislation of the "general or national government" of "a nation *de facto*." The most important measures of general concern are rested upon no stronger foundation than "the sacred ties of virtue, honor and the love of our country," and have no higher sanction than public contempt and exclusion from the ordinary intercourse of society!

A Brief Inquiry into the True Nature and Character of Our Federal Government
by Abel P. Upshur (1840)

would have been an act of open rebellion, and would have severed at once all the ties which bound them to the mother country, and which they were still anxious to preserve. New York was represented in this congress precisely as she had been in the former one, that is, by delegates chosen by a part of her people; for the royal party was so strong in that colony, that it would have been impossible to obtain from the legislature an expression of approbation of any measure of resistance to British authority. The accession of Georgia to the general association was not made known till the 20th of July, and her delegates did not take their seats till the 13th of September. In the meantime congress had proceeded in the discharge of its duties, and some of its most important acts, and among the rest the appointment of a commander-in-chief of their armies, were performed while those two colonies were unrepresented. Its acts, like those of the former congress, were in the form of resolution and recommendation; for as it still held out the hope of reconciliation with the parent country, it did not venture to assume the function of authoritative legislation. It continued to hold this attitude and to act in this mode till the 4th of July, 1776, when it declared that the colonies there represented (including New York, which had acceded after the battle of Lexington), were, and of right ought to be, free and independent States.*

---

* That the powers granted to the delegates to the second congress were substantially the same with those granted to the delegates to the first, will appear from the following extracts from their credentials.

New Hampshire. "To consent and agree to all measures, which said congress shall deem necessary to obtain redress of American grievances." Delegates appointed by a *convention*.

Massachusetts. "To concert, agree upon, direct and order" (in concert with the delegates of the other colonies) "such further measures as to them shall appear to be best calculated for the recovery and establishment of American rights and liberties, and for restoring harmony between Great Britain and the colonies." Delegates appointed by provincial congress.

Connecticut. "To join, consult and advise with the other colonies in British America, on proper measures for advancing the best good of the colonies." Delegates appointed by the colonial house of representatives.

The *colony* of New York was not represented in this congress, but delegates were appointed by a convention of deputies from the city and county of New York, the city and county of Albany and the counties of Dutchess, Ulster, Orange, West Chester, King's and Suffolk. They gave their delegates power to "concert and determine upon such measures, as shall be judged most effectual for the preservation and re-establishment of American rights and privileges,

It is to be remarked, that no new powers were conferred on congress after the declaration of independence. Strictly speaking, they had

---

and for the restoration of harmony between Great Britain and the colonies." Queen's county approved of the proceeding.

Pennsylvania. Simply to "attend the general congress." Delegates appointed by provincial assembly.

New Jersey. "To attend the continental congress and to report their proceedings to the next session of general assembly." Delegates appointed by the colonial assembly.

Delaware. "To concert and agree upon such farther measures, as shall appear to them best calculated for the accommodation of the unhappy differences between Great Britain and the colonies on a constitutional foundation, which the house most ardently wish for, and that they report their proceedings to the next session of general assembly." Delegates appointed by the assembly.

Maryland. "To consent and agree to all measures, which said congress shall deem necessary and effectual to obtain a redress of American grievances; and this province bind themselves to execute, to the utmost of their power, all resolutions which the said congress may adopt." Delegates appointed by convention, and subsequently approved by the general assembly.

Virginia. "To represent this colony in general congress, to be held, &c." Delegates appointed by convention.

North Carolina. "Such powers as may make any acts done by them, or any of them, or consent given in behalf of this province, obligatory in honor upon every inhabitant thereof." Delegates appointed by convention, and approved in general assembly.

South Carolina. "To concert, agree to and effectually prosecute such measures, as in the opinion of the said deputies, and the deputies to be assembled, shall be most likely to obtain a redress of American grievances." Delegates appointed by provincial congress.

In the copy of the Journals of Congress now before me I do not find the credentials of the delegates from Rhode Island. They did not attend at the first meeting of congress, although they did at a subsequent period. Georgia was not represented in this congress until September, 1775. On the 13th May, 1775, Lyman Hall appeared as a delegate from the parish of St. Johns, and he was admitted to his seat, "subject to such regulations, as the congress shall determine, relative to his voting." He was never regarded as the representative of Georgia, nor was that colony then considered as a party to the proceedings of congress. This is evident from the fact that, in the address to the inhabitants of Great Britain, they use the style, "The *twelve* United Colonies, by their delegates in congress, to the inhabitants of Great Britain," adopted on the 8th July, 1775. On the 20th of that month congress were notified that a convention of Georgia had appointed delegates to attend them, but none of them took their seats till the 13th September following. They were authorized "to do, transact, join and concur with the several delegates from the other colonies and provinces upon this continent, on all such matters and things as shall appear eligible and fit, at this alarming time, for the preservation and defense of our rights and liberties, and for the restoration of harmony, upon constitutional principles, between Great Britain and America."

Some of the colonies appointed their delegates only for limited times, at the expiration of which they were replaced by others, but without any material change in their powers. The delegates were, in all things, subject to the orders of their respective colonies.

A Brief Inquiry into the True Nature and Character of Our Federal Government
by Abel P. Upshur (1840)

no authority to make that declaration. They were not appointed for any such purpose, but precisely the reverse; and although some of them were expressly authorized to agree to it, yet others were not. Indeed, we are informed by Mr. Jefferson, that the declaration was opposed by some of the firmest patriots of the body, and among the rest, by R. R. Livingston, Dickenson, Wilson and E. Rutledge, on the ground that it was premature; that the people of New York, New Jersey, Maryland and Delaware were not *yet ripe for it*, but would soon unite with the rest, if not indiscreetly urged. In venturing upon so bold a step, congress acted precisely as they did in all other cases, in the name of the States whose representatives they were, and with a full reliance that those States would confirm whatever they might do for the general good. They were, strictly, agents or ministers of independent States, acting each under the authority and instructions of his own State, and having no power whatever, except what those instructions conferred. The States themselves were not bound by the resolves of congress, except so far as they respectively authorized their own delegates to bind them. There was no original grant of powers to that body, except for deliberation and advisement; there was no constitution, no law, no agreement, to which they could refer, in order to ascertain the extent of their powers. The members did not all act under the same instructions, nor with the same extent of authority. The different States gave different instructions, each according to its own views of right and policy, and without reference to any general scheme to which they were all bound to conform. Congress had in fact *no power of government at all*, nor had it that character of *permanency* which is implied in the idea of government. It could not pass an obligatory law, nor devise an obligatory sanction, by virtue of any inherent power in itself. It was, as already remarked, precisely the same body *after* the declaration of independence as *before*. As it was not then a government, and could not establish any new and valid relations between the colonies, so long as they acknowledged themselves dependencies of the British crown, they certainly could not do so after the declaration of independence, without some new grant of power. The dependent colonies had then become independent States; their political condition and relations were necessarily changed by that circumstance; the deliberative and advisory body, through whom they had consulted together as colonies, was *functus officio*; the authority which appointed them had ceased to exist, or was superseded by a higher authority. Everything which they did, after this period and before the articles of confederation, was without any other right or authority than what was derived from the mere consent and acquiescence of the several States. In the ordinary business of that government *de facto*, which the occasion had called into existence, they did whatever the public interest seemed to require, upon the secure reliance that their acts would be approved and confirmed. In other cases, however, they called for specific grants of power; and in such cases, each representative applied to his own State alone, and not to any other State or people. Indeed, as they were called into existence by the *colonies* in 1775, and as they continued in existence, without any new election or new grant of power, it is difficult to perceive how they could form a "general or national government, organized by *the people*." They were *elected* by subjects of the king of England; subjects who had no right, as they themselves admitted, to establish any government whatever; and when those subjects became citizens of independent states, they gave no instructions to establish any such government. The government *exercised* was, as already remarked, merely a government *de facto*, and no farther *de jure* than the subsequent approval of its acts by the several States made it so.

This brief review will enable us to determine how far the author is supported in the inferences he has drawn, in the passages last quoted. We have reason to regret that in these, as in many others, he has not been sufficiently specific, either in stating his proposition or in citing his proof. To what people does he allude, when he tells us that the "first general or national government" was organized "by the people"? The first and every recommendation to send deputies to a general congress was addressed to the colonies *as such*; in the choice of those deputies each colony acted for itself, without mingling in any way with the people or government of any other colony; and when the deputies met in congress, they voted on all questions of public and general concern by colonies, each colony having one vote, whatever was its population or number of deputies. If, then, this government was organized by "the people" at all, it was clearly the people of the *several* colonies, and not the *joint* people of *all* the colonies. And where is the author's warrant for the assertion, that they acted "directly in their primary sovereign capacity, and without the intervention of the functionaries, to whom the ordinary powers of government were delegated in the colonies"? He is in most respects a close follower of Marshall, and he could scarcely have failed to see the following passage, which is found in a note in the 168th page of the second volume of the Life of Washington. Speaking of the Congress of 1774, Marshall says: "The members of this congress were *generally* elected by the authority of the colonial legislatures, but in *some* instances a different system had been pursued. In New Jersey and Maryland the elections were made by committees chosen in the several counties for that particular purpose; and in New York, where the royal party was very strong, and where it is probable that no legislative act, authorizing an election of members to represent that colony in congress, could have been obtained, the people themselves assembled in those places, where the spirit of opposition to the claims of parliament prevailed, and elected deputies, who were very readily received into Congress." Here the *general rule* is stated to be, that the deputies were elected by the "colonial legislatures," and the instances in which the people acted "directly in their primary, sovereign capacity, without the intervention of the ordinary functionaries of government," are given as *exceptions*. And even in those cases, in which delegates were appointed by conventions of the people, it was deemed necessary in many instances, as we have already seen, that the appointment should be approved and confirmed by the ordinary legislature, As to New York, neither her people nor her government had so far lost their attachment to the mother country as to concur in any measure of opposition until after the battle of Lexington in April, 1775; and the only representatives which New York had in the congress of 1774 were those of a comparatively small portion of her people. It is well known – and, indeed, the author himself so informs us –

that the members of the congress of 1775 were elected substantially as were those of the preceding congress; so that there were very few of the colonies, in which the people performed that act in their "primary, sovereign capacity," without the intervention of their constituted authorities. It is of little consequence, however, to the present inquiry, whether the deputies were chosen by the colonial legislatures, as was done in most of the colonies, or by conventions, as was done in Georgia and some others, or by committees appointed for the purpose, as was done in one or two instances, or by the people in primary assemblies, as was done in *part* of New York. All these modes were resorted to, according as the one or the other appeared most convenient or proper in each particular case. But, whichever mode was adopted, the members were chosen by each colony in and for itself, and were the representatives of *that* colony alone, and not of any other colony, or any nation *de facto* or *de jure*. The assertion, therefore, that "the congress thus assembled exercised *de facto* and *de jure* a sovereign authority, not as the delegated agents of the government *de facto* of the colonies, but in virtue of original powers derived from the people," is, to say the least of it, *very* bold, in one who had undoubtedly explored all the sources of information upon the subject. Until the adoption of the articles of confederation congress had no "original powers," except only for deliberation and advisement, and claimed no "sovereign authority" whatever. It was an occasional, and not a permanent body, or one renewable from time to time. Although they did, in many instances, "exercise *de facto*" a power of legislation to a certain extent, yet they never held that power "*de jure*," by any grant from the colonies or the people; and their acts became valid only by subsequent confirmation of them, and not because they had any delegated authority to perform them. The whole history of the period proves this, and not a single instance can be cited to the contrary. The course of the revolutionary government throughout attests the fact, that, however the people may have occasionally acted, in pressing emergencies, without the intervention of the authorities of their respective colonial governments, they never lost sight of the fact that they were citizens of separate colonies, and never, even impliedly, surrendered that character, or acknowledged a different allegiance. In all the acts of congress, reference was had to the colonies, and never to the people. That body had no power to act directly upon the people, and could not execute its own resolves as to most purposes, except by the aid and intervention of the colonial authorities. Its measures were adopted by the votes of the colonies *as such*, and not by the rule of mere numerical majority, which prevails in every legislative assembly of an entire nation. This fact alone is decisive to prove, that the members were not the representatives of the people of *all* the colonies, for the judgment of each colony was pronounced by its *own* members only, and no others had any right to mingle in their deliberations. What, then, was this "sovereign authority"? What was the nature, what the extent, of its "original powers"? From what "people" were these powers derived? I look in vain for answers to these questions to any historical record which has yet met my view, and have only to regret that the author has not directed me to better guides.

{Chapter IV}

The author's conclusion is not better sustained by the nature and extent of the powers *exercised* by the revolutionary government. It has already been stated, that no original powers of legislation were granted to the congresses of 1774 and 1775; and it is only from their acts that we can determine what powers they actually exercised. The circumstances under which they were called into existence precluded the possibility of any precise limitations of their powers, even if it had been designed to clothe them with the functions of government. The colonies were suffering under common oppressions, and were threatened with common dangers, from the mother country. The great object which they had in view was to produce that concert of action among themselves which would best enable them to resist their common enemy, and best secure the safety and liberties of all. Great confidence must necessarily be reposed in public rulers under circumstances of this sort. We may well suppose, therefore, that the revolutionary government exercised every power which appeared to be necessary for the successful prosecution of the great contest in which they were engaged; and we may, with equal propriety, suppose that neither the people nor the colonial governments felt any disposition to scrutinize very narrowly any measure which promised protection and safety to themselves. They knew that the government was temporary only; that it was permitted only for a particular and temporary object, and that they could at any time recall any and every power which it had assumed. It would be a violent and forced inference, from the powers of such an *agency*, (for it was not a government, although I have sometimes, for convenience, called it so), however great they might be, to say that the people, or States, which established it, meant thereby to merge their distinctive character, to surrender all the rights and privileges which belonged to them as separate communities, and to consolidate themselves into one nation.

In point of fact, however, there was nothing in the powers exercised by the revolutionary government, so far as they can be known from their acts, inconsistent with the perfect sovereignty and independence of the States. These were always admitted in *terms*, and were never denied in *practice*. So far as external relations were concerned, congress seems to have exercised every power of a supreme government. They assumed the right to "declare war and to make peace; to authorize captures; to institute appellate prize courts; to direct and control all national, military and naval operations; to form alliances and make treaties; to contract debts and issue bills of credit on national account." These powers were not "exclusive," however, as our author supposes. On the contrary, troops were raised, vessels of war were commissioned, and various military operations were conducted by the colonies, on their own separate means and authority. Ticonderoga was taken by the troops of Connecticut before the declaration of independence; Massachusetts and Connecticut fitted out armed vessels to cruise against those of England, in October, 1775; South Carolina soon followed their example. In 1776, New Hampshire authorized her executive to issue letters of marque and reprisal.

These instances are selected out of many, as sufficient to show that in the conduct of war congress possessed no "exclusive" power, and that the colonies (or States) retained, and actually asserted, their own sovereign right and power as to that matter. And not as to that matter alone, for New Hampshire established post offices. The words of our author may, indeed, import that the power of congress over the subject of war was "exclusive" only as to such military and naval operations as he considers national, that is, such as were undertaken by the joint power of all the colonies; and, if so, he is correct. But the comma after the word "national" suggests a different interpretation. At all events, the facts which I have mentioned prove that congress exercised no power which was considered as abridging the absolute sovereignty and independence of the States.

Many of those powers which, for greater convenience, were entrusted exclusively to congress, could not be effectually exerted except by the aid of the State authorities. The troops required by congress were raised by the States, and the commissions of their officers were countersigned by the governors of the States. Congress were allowed to issue bills of credit, but they could not make them a legal tender, nor punish the counterfeiter of them. Neither could they bind the States to redeem them, nor raise by their own authority the necessary funds for that purpose. Congress received ambassadors and other public ministers, yet they had no power to extend to them that protection which they receive from the government of every sovereign nation. A man by the name of De Longchamps entered the house of the French minister plenipotentiary in Philadelphia, and there threatened violence to the person of Francis Barbe Marbois, secretary of the French legation, consul general of France, and consul for the state of Pennsylvania; he afterwards assaulted and beat him in the public street. For this offence, he was indicted and tried in *the court of Oyer and Terminer of Philadelphia*, and punished under its sentence. The case turned chiefly upon the law of nations, with reference to the protection which it secures to foreign ministers. A question was made, whether *the authorities of Pennsylvania* should not deliver up De Longchamps to the French government to be dealt with at their pleasure. It does not appear that the federal government was considered to possess any power over the subject, or that it was deemed proper to invoke its counsel or authority in any form. This case occurred in 1784, after the adoption of the articles of confederation; but if the powers of the federal government were *less* under those articles than before, it only proves that, however great its previous powers may have been, they were held at the will of the States, and were actually recalled by the articles of confederation. Thus it appears that, in the important functions of raising an army, of providing a public revenue, of paying public debts, and giving security to the persons of foreign ministers, the boasted "sovereignty" of the federal government was merely nominal, and owed its entire efficiency to the co-operation and aid of the State governments. Congress had no power to coerce those governments; nor could it exercise any direct authority over their individual citizens.

Although the powers actually assumed and exercised by congress were certainly very great, they were not always acquiesced in, or allowed, by the States. Thus, the power to lay an embargo was earnestly desired by them, but was denied by the States. And in order the more clearly to indicate that many of their powers were exercised merely by sufferance, and at the same time to lend a sanction to their authority so far as they chose to allow it, it was deemed necessary, by at least *one* of the States, to pass laws indemnifying those who might act in obedience to the resolutions of that body.*

A conclusive proof, however, of the true relation which the colonies held to the revolutionary government, even in the opinion of congress itself, is furnished by their own journals. In June, 1776, that body recommended the passing of laws for the punishment of treason; and they declare that the crime shall be considered as committed against *the colonies individually*, and not against them all, as united or confederated together. This could scarcely have been so, if they had considered themselves "a government *de facto* and *de jure*," clothed with "sovereign authority." The author, however, is not satisfied to rest his opinion upon historical facts; he seeks also to fortify himself by a judicial decision. He informs us that, "soon after the organization of the present government, the question [of the powers of the continental congress] was most elaborately discussed before the supreme court of the United States, in a case calling for an exposition of the appellate jurisdiction of congress in prize causes, before the ratification of the confederation. The result of that examination was, that congress before the confederation possessed, by the *consent of the people of the United States*, sovereign and supreme powers for national purposes; and, among others, the supreme powers of peace and war, and, as an incident, the right of entertaining appeals in the last resort, in prize causes, even in opposition to State legislation. And that the actual powers exercised by congress, in respect to national objects, furnished the best exposition of its constitutional authority, since they emanated from *the people*, and were acquiesced in by *the people*."

---

* This was done by Pennsylvania. — See 2 *Dallas, Col. K. of Penn. 3.*

There is in this passage great want of accuracy, and perhaps some want of candor. The author, as usual, neglects to cite the judicial decision to which he alludes, but it must be the case of Penhallow and others against Doane's administrators. (3 Dallas' Reports, 54.) Congress, in November, 1775, passed a resolution, recommending to the several colonies to establish prize courts, with a right of appeal from their decisions to congress. In 1776, New Hampshire accordingly passed a law upon the subject, by which an appeal to congress was allowed in cases of capture by vessels in the service of the united colonies; but where the capture was made by "a vessel in the service of the united colonies and of any particular colony or person together," the appeal was allowed to the superior court of New Hampshire. The brigantine Susanna was captured by a vessel owned and commanded by citizens of New Hampshire, and was duly condemned as prize by her own court of admiralty. An appeal was prayed to congress and denied; and thereupon an appeal to the superior court of New Hampshire was prayed and allowed. From the decision of this court an appeal was taken to congress, in the mode prescribed by their resolution, and the case was disposed of by the court of appeals, appointed by congress to take cognizance of such cases. After the adoption of the present constitution and the organization of the judiciary system under it, a libel was filed in the district court of New Hampshire, to carry into effect the sentence of the court of appeals above-mentioned. The cause being legally transferred to the circuit court, was decided there, and an appeal allowed to the supreme court. That court, in its decision, sustains the jurisdiction of the court of appeals established by congress. Mr. Justice Patterson's opinion is founded mainly upon these grounds: That the powers actually exercised by congress ought to be considered as legitimate, because they were such as the occasion absolutely required, and were approved and acquiesced in by "the people"; that the authority ultimately and finally to decide on all matters and questions touching the law of nations does reside and is vested in the sovereign supreme power of war and peace; that this power was lodged in the continental congress by the consent and acquiescence of "the people"; that the legality of all captures on the high seas must be determined by the law of nations; that New Hampshire had committed herself upon this subject by voting in favor of the exercise of the same power by congress in the case of the brig Active; that as the commission, under which the capture in the case under consideration was made, was issued by congress, it resulted, of necessity, that the validity of all captures made by virtue of that commission should be judged of by congress, or its constituted authority, because "everyone must be amenable to the authority under which he acts." It is evident that this opinion, while it sustains the authority of congress in the particular case, does not prove its general supremacy, nor that the States had surrendered to it any part of their sovereignty and independence. On the contrary, it affirms that the "sovereign and supreme power of war and peace" was *assumed* by congress, and that the exercise of it became legitimate, only because it was approved and acquiesced in; and that being thus legitimated, the appellate jurisdiction in prize cases followed as a necessary incident. All the powers, which Patterson contends for as exercised by congress, may well be conceded, without in the slightest degree affecting the question before us; they were as consistent with the character of a federative, as with that of a consolidated government. He does not tell us to what people he alludes, when he says that the powers exercised by congress were approved and ratified by "the people." He does not, in any part of his opinion, authorize the idea of the author, that "congress possessed, before the confederation, by the consent of *the people of the United States*, sovereign and supreme powers for national purposes." On the contrary, as to one of those powers, he holds the opposite language; and therefore it is fair to presume, that he intended to be so understood in regard to all the rest. This is his language: "The authority exercised by congress, in granting commissions to privateers, was approved and ratified by *the several colonies or states*, because they received and filled up the commissions and bonds, and returned the latter to congress." This approval and ratification alone rendered, in his opinion, the exercise of this, and other similar powers assumed by congress, legitimate.

Judge Iredell, in delivering his opinion, goes much more fully into the examination of the powers of the revolutionary government. He thinks that, as the power of peace and war was entrusted to congress, they held, as a necessary incident, the power to establish prize courts; and that whatever powers they did in fact exercise, were acquiesced in and consented to, and, consequently, legitimated and confirmed. But he leaves no room to doubt as to the source whence this confirmation was derived. After proving that the several colonies were, to all intents and purposes, separate and distinct, and that they did not form "one people" in any sense of the term, he says, "if congress, previous to the articles of confederation, possessed any authority, it was an authority, as I have shown, derived from the people of each province, in the first instance." "The authority was not possessed by congress, unless given by all the States." "I conclude, therefore, that every particle of authority, which originally resided either in congress or in any branch of the State governments, was derived from the people who were permanent inhabitants of each province, in the first instance, and afterwards became citizens of each State; that this authority was conveyed by each body politic separately, *and not by all the people in the several provinces or states* jointly." No language could be stronger than this, to disaffirm the author's conclusion, that the powers exercised by congress were exercised "by the consent of *the people of the United States.*" Certainly, Iredell did not think so.

The other two judges, Blair and Cushing, affirm the general propositions upon which Paterson and Iredell sustained the power of congress in the particular case, but lend no support to the idea of any such unity among the people of the several colonies or states, as our author supposes to have existed. Cushing, without formally discussing the question, expressly says that "he has no doubt of the sovereignty of the States."

This decision, then, merely affirms, what no one has ever thought of denying, that the revolutionary government exercised every power which the occasion required; that, among these, the powers of peace and war were most important, because congress, alone, represented *all* the colonies, and could, alone, express the general will, and wield the general strength; that wherever the powers of peace and war are lodged, belongs also the right to decide all questions touching the laws of nations; that prize causes are of this character; and, finally, that all these powers were not derived from any original grant, but are to be considered as belonging to congress, *merely because congress exercised them*, and because they were sustained in so doing by the approbation of the several colonies or states, whose representatives they were. Surely, then, our author was neither very accurate nor very candid, in so stating this decision as to give rise to the idea that, in the opinion of the supreme court, congress possessed original sovereign powers, by the consent of "the people of the United States." Even, however, if the court had so decided, in express terms, it would have been of no value in the present inquiry, as will by-and-by be shown.

The examination of this part of the subject has probably been already drawn out to too great an extent; but it would not be complete without some notice of another ground, upon which our author rests his favorite idea – that the people of the colonies formed "one people," or nation. Even if this unity was not produced by the appointment of the revolutionary government, or by the nature of the powers exercised by them, and acquiesced in by the people, he thinks there can be no doubt that this was the necessary result of the declaration of independence. In order that he may be fully understood upon this point, I will transcribe the entire passage relating to it.

"In the next place, the colonies did not severally act for themselves, and proclaim their own independence. It is true that some of the States had previously formed incipient governments for themselves; but it was done in compliance with the recommendations of congress. Virginia, on the 29th of June, 1776, by a convention of delegates, declared 'the government of this country, as formerly exercised under the crown of Great Britain, totally dissolved,' and proceeded to form a new constitution of government. New Hampshire also formed a new government, in December, 1775, which was manifestly intended to be temporary, 'during (as they said) the unhappy and unnatural contest with Great Britain.' New

Jersey, too, established a frame of government, on the 2nd July, 1776; but it was expressly declared that it should be void upon a reconciliation with Great Britain. And South Carolina, in March, 1776, adopted a constitution of government; but this was in like manner 'established until an accommodation between Great Britain and America could be obtained.' But the declaration of the independence of all the colonies was the united act of all. It was 'a declaration by the representatives of the United States of America, in congress assembled;' 'by the delegates appointed by the good people of the colonies,' as, in a prior declaration of rights, they were called. It was not an act done by the State governments then organized, nor by persons chosen by them. It was emphatically the act of the whole *people* of the united colonies, by the instrumentality of their representatives, chosen for that, among other purposes. It was an act not competent to the State governments, or any of them, as organized under their charters, to adopt. Those charters neither contemplated the case nor provided for it. It was an act of original, inherent sovereignty by the people themselves, resulting from their right to change the form of government, and to institute a new government, whenever necessary for their safety and happiness. So the declaration of independence treats it. No State had presumed, of itself, to form a new government, or provide for the exigencies of the times, without consulting congress on the subject; and when they acted, it was in pursuance of the recommendation of congress. It was, therefore, the achievement of the whole, for the benefit of the whole. The people of the united colonies made the united colonies free and independent states, and absolved them from allegiance to the British crown. The declaration of independence has, accordingly, always been treated as an act of paramount and sovereign authority, complete and perfect *per se*; and *ipso facto* working an entire dissolution of all political connection with, and allegiance to, Great Britain. And this, not merely as a practical fact, but in a legal and constitutional view of the matter by courts of justice."

The first question which this passage naturally suggests to the mind of the reader is this: if two or more nations or people, confessedly separate, distinct and independent, each having its own peculiar government, without any "direct political connection with each other," yet owing the same allegiance to one common superior, should unite in a declaration of rights which they believed belonged to all of them alike, would that circumstance, alone, make them "one people"? Stripped of the circumstances with which the author has surrounded it, this is, at last, the only proposition involved. If Spain, Naples and Holland, while they were "dependencies" of the imperial crown of France, had united in declaring that they were oppressed, in the same mode and degree, by the measures of that crown, and that they did, for that reason, disclaim all allegiance to it, and assume the station of "free and independent states," would they thereby have become one people? Surely this will not be asserted by anyone. We should see, in that act, nothing more than the union of several independent sovereignties, for the purpose of effecting a common object, which each felt itself too weak to effect, alone. Nothing would be more natural, than that nations so situated should establish a common military power, a common treasury, and a common agency, through which to carry on their intercourse with other powers; but that all this should unite them together, so as to form them into one nation, is a consequence not readily perceived. The case here supposed is precisely that of the American colonies, if those colonies were, in point of fact, separate, distinct, and independent of one another. If they were so, (and I think it has been shown that they were), then the fact that they united in the declaration of independence does not make them "one people," any more than a similar declaration would have made Spain, Naples and Holland one people; if they were not so, then they were one people already, and the declaration of independence did not render them either more or less identical. It is true, the analogy here supposed does not hold in every particular; the relations of the colonies to one another were certainly closer, in many respects, than those of Spain, Naples and Holland, to one another. But as to all purposes involved in the present inquiry, the analogy is perfect. The effect attributed to the declaration of independence presupposes that the colonies were not "one people" before; an effect which is in no manner changed or modified by any other circumstance in their relation to one another. That fact, alone, is necessary to be inquired into; and until that fact is ascertained, the author's reasoning as to the effect of the declaration of independence, in making them "one people," does not apply. He is obliged, therefore, to abandon the ground previously taken, to wit, that the colonies were one people *before* the declaration of independence. And having abandoned it, he places the colonies, as to this question, upon the footing of any other separate and distinct nations; and, as to these, it is quite evident that the conclusion which he has drawn, in the case of the colonies, could not be correct, unless it would be equally correct in the case of Spain, Naples and Holland, above supposed.

{Chapter V}

The mere fact, then, that the colonies united in the declaration of independence, did not *necessarily* make them one people. But it may be said that this fact ought, at least, to be received as proof that they considered themselves as one people already. The argument is fair, and I freely let it go for what it is worth. The opinion of the congress of 1775, whatever it may have been, and however strongly expressed, could not possibly change the historical facts. It depended upon those facts, alone, whether the colonies were one people or not. They might by their agreement, expressed through their agents in congress, make themselves one people through all time to come; but their power, as to this matter, could not extend to the time past. Indeed, it is contended, not only by our author, but by others, that the colonies did, *by and in that act*, agree to become "one people" for the future. They suppose that such agreement is implied, if not expressed, in the following passages. "We, therefore, the representatives of the United States of America," "do, in the name and by the authority of the good people of these colonies, solemnly publish and declare that these united colonies are, and of right ought to be, free and independent states." Let us test the correctness of this opinion, by the history of the time, and by the rules of fair criticism.

The congress of 1775, by which independence was declared, was appointed, as has been before shown, by the colonies in their separate and distinct capacity, each acting for itself, and not conjointly with any other. They were the representatives, each of his own colony, and not of any other; each had authority to act in the name of his own colony, and not in that of any other; each colony gave its own vote by its own representatives, and not by those of any other colony. Of course, it was as separate and distinct colonies that they deliberated on the declaration of independence. When, therefore, they declare, in the adoption of that measure, that they act as "the representatives of the United States of America," and "in the name and by the authority of the good people of these colonies," they must of course be understood as speaking in the character in which they had all along acted; that is, as the representatives of separate and distinct colonies, and not as the joint representatives of any one people. A decisive proof of this is found in the fact that the colonies voted on the adoption of that measure in their separate character, each giving one vote by all its own representatives, who acted in strict obedience to specific instructions from their respective colonies, and the members signed the declaration in that way. So, also, when they declared that "these united colonies are, and of right ought to be, free and independent states," they meant only that their respective communities, which until then had been dependent colonies, should thereafter be independent states, and that the same union, which existed between them as colonies, should be continued between them as states. The measure under consideration looked only to their relation to the mother country, and not to their relation to one another; and the sole question before them was, whether they should continue in a state of dependence on the British crown, or not. Having determined that they would not, they from that moment ceased to be colonies, and became states; united, precisely as before, for the common purpose of achieving their common liberty. The idea of forming a closer union, by the mere act of declaring themselves independent, could scarcely have occurred to any one of them. The necessity of such a measure must have been apparent to all, and it had long before engaged their attention in a different form. Men, of their wisdom and forecast, meditating a measure so necessary to their common safety, would not have left it as a mere matter of *inference* from another measure. In point of fact, it was already before them, in the form of a distinct proposition, and had been so ever since their first meeting in May, 1775.* It is impossible to suppose therefore,

---

* A document which I have not met with elsewhere, but which may be found in the Appendix to Professor Tucker's elaborate and instructive Life of Jefferson, affords important evidence upon this point. As early as May, 1775, the plan of a "confederation and perpetual union" among the colonies, was prepared and proposed for adoption. It was not in fact adopted, but its provisions show, in the strongest manner, in what light the colonies regarded their relation to one another. The proposed union was called "a firm *league* of friendship"; each colony reserved to itself "as much as it might think proper of its own present laws, customs, rights, privileges and peculiar jurisdictions, within its own limits; and may amend its own constitution as may seem best to its own assembly or convention"; the external relations of the colonies were to be managed by their general government alone, and all amendments of

A Brief Inquiry into the True Nature and Character of Our Federal Government
by Abel P. Upshur (1840)

in common justice to the sagacity of congress, that they meant anything more by the declaration of independence, than simply to sever the tie which had theretofore bound them to England, and to assert the rights of the separate and distinct colonies, as separate and independent States; particularly as the language which they use is fairly susceptible of this construction. The instrument itself is entitled, "the unanimous declaration of the thirteen United States of America"; of *States*, separate and distinct bodies politic, and not of "one people" or nation, composed of all of them together; "united," as independent States may be, by compact or agreement, and not *amalgamated*, as they would be, if they formed *one* nation or body politic.

Is it true then, as the author supposes, that the "colonies did not severally act for themselves, and proclaim their own independence"? It is true that they acted *together*; but is it not equally true that each *acted for itself alone*, without pretending to any right or authority to bind any other? Their declaration was simply their *joint expression* of their separate wills; each expressing its own will, and not that of any other; each bound by its own act, and not responsible for the act of any other. If the colonies had severally declared their independence through their own legislatures, and had afterwards agreed to unite their forces together to make a common cause of their contest, and to submit their common interests to the management of a common council chosen by themselves, wherein would their situation have been different? And is it true that this declaration of independence "was not an act done by the State governments then organized, nor

---

their "constitution," as they termed it, were to be proposed by congress and "approved by a majority of the colony assemblies." It can scarcely be contended that this "league of friendship," this "confederation and perpetual union," would, if it had been adopted, have rendered the people of the several colonies less identical than they were before. If, in their own opinion, they were "one people" already, no league or confederation was necessary, and no one would have thought of proposing it. The very fact, therefore, that it was proposed, as a necessary measure "for their common defense against their enemies, for the security of their liberties and their properties, the safety of their persons and families, and their mutual and general welfare," proves that they did not consider themselves as already "one people," in any sense or to any extent which would enable them to effect those important objects.

This proposition was depending and undetermined at the time of the declaration of independence.

by persons chosen by them"? That "it was emphatically the act of the whole *people* of the united colonies, by the instrumentality of their representatives chosen for that among other purposes"? What representatives were those that were chosen by "the people of the united colonies"? When and how were they chosen? Those who declared the colonies independent were chosen more than a year before that event; they were chosen by the colonies separately, and, as has already been shown, through the instrumentality of their own "governments then organized"; they were chosen, not for the "purpose" of declaring the colonies independent, but of protecting them against oppression, and bringing about a reconciliation with the parent country, upon fair terms, if possible. (Jefferson's Notes, 1st ed. 128, 129.) If there were any other representatives than these concerned in the declaration of independence, if that act was performed by representatives chosen by "the whole people of the colonies"; for that or any other purpose, if any such representatives *could possibly have been chosen* by the colonies as then organized, no historical record, that has yet met my view, contains one syllable of the matter.

The author seems to attach but little importance to the fact, that several of the colonies had established separate governments for themselves, prior to the declaration of independence. He regards this as of little consequence; because he thinks that the colonies so acted only in pursuance of the recommendation of congress, and would not have "presumed" to do it, "without consulting congress upon the subject"; and because the governments so established were, for the most part, designed to be temporary, and to continue only during the contest with England. Such recommendation was given in express terms, to New Hampshire and South Carolina, in November, 1775, and to Virginia, in December of that year; and on the 10th May, 1776, "it was resolved to *recommend* to the respective assemblies and conventions of the united colonies where no government sufficient to the exigencies of their affairs had been established, to adopt such a government as should, in the opinion of the representatives of the people, best conduce to the happiness and safety of their constituents in particular, and of America in general." The preamble to this resolution was not adopted till the 15th May. (1 Elliott's Debates, 80, 83.) It is evident, from the language here employed, that congress claimed no power over the colonies as to this matter, and no right to influence or control them in the exercise of the important function of forming their own governments. It *recommended* only; and, contemplating the colonies as separate and distinct, referred it to the assembly or convention of each, to establish any form of government which might be acceptable to its own people. Of what consequence was it, whether the colonies acted upon the recommendation and advice of others, or merely upon their own will and counsels? With whatever *motive* the act was performed, it was one of supreme and sovereign power, and such as could not have been performed except by a sovereign people. And whether the government so established was intended to last forever, or only for a limited time, did not affect its character as an act of sovereign power. In point of fact, then, the colonies which established such governments did, by that very act, assert their sovereignty and independence. They had no power, under their charters, to change their governments. They could do so only by setting their charters aside, and acting upon their inherent, sovereign right: and this was *revolution*. In effect, therefore, many of the colonies had declared their independence prior to the 4th July, 1776; they had commenced the revolution, and were considered by England as in a state of rebellion. Of Virginia this is emphatically true. Her declaration of rights was made on the 12th of June, 1776; and her constitution was adopted on the 29th of the same month. This constitution continued until 1829. Her subsequent declaration of independence, on the 4th of July, in common with the other colonies, was but a more public, though not a more solemn affirmation of what she had previously done; a pledge to the whole world, that what she had resolved on in her separate character, she would unite with the other colonies in performing. She could not declare herself free and independent more distinctly, in that form, than she had already done, by asserting her sovereign and irresponsible power, in throwing off her former government, and establishing a new one for herself.*

* In point of fact, Virginia declared her independence on the *15th of May*, 1776. The following beautiful allusion to that scene is extracted from an address delivered by Judge Beverly Tucker, of William and Mary College, before the Petersburg Lyceum, on the 15th May, 1839.

"That spectacle, on this day sixty-three years, Virginia exhibited to the world; and the memory of that majestic scene it is now my task to rescue from oblivion. It was on that day that she renounced her colonial dependence on Great Britain, and separated herself forever from that kingdom. Then it was that, bursting the manacles of a foreign tyranny, she, in the same moment, imposed upon herself the salutary restrains of law and order. In that moment she commenced the work of forming a government, complete within itself; and having perfected that work, she, on the 29th of June in the same year, performed the highest function of independent sovereignty, by adopting, ordaining and establishing the constitution under which all of us were born. Then it was that, sufficient to herself for all the purposes of government, she prescribed that oath of fealty and allegiance to her sole and separate sovereignty, which all of us, who have held any office under her authority, have solemnly called upon the Searcher of hearts to witness and record. In that hour, gentlemen, it could not be certainly known, that the other colonies would take the same decisive step. It was, indeed, expected. In the same breath in which she had declared her own independence, Virginia had advised it. She had instructed her delegates in the general congress to urge it; and it was by the voice of one of her sons, whose name will ever proudly live in her history, that the word of power was spoken, at which the chain that bound the colonies to the parent kingdom fell asunder, 'as flax that severs at the touch of fire.' But even then and while the terms of the *general* declaration of independence were yet unsettled, hers had already gone forth. The voice of her defiance was already ringing in the tyrant's ears; hers was the cry that summoned him to the strife; hers was the shout that invited his vengeance: '*Me! me! Adsum qui feci; in me, convertite ferrum.*'"

This beautiful address, abounding in patriotic sentiments, and sound political doctrines, clothed in the richest language, ought to be in the hands of every citizen, and particularly of those of Virginia. The following extract from the Journals of the Convention, containing the history of this interesting event, cannot fail to be acceptable to every American reader.

"*Wednesday, May 15th*, 1776. — The convention, then, according to the order of the day, resolved itself into a committee on the state of the colony; and, after some time spent therein, Mr. President resumed the chair, and Mr. Cary reported that the committee had, according to order, had under their consideration the state of the colony, and had come to the following resolutions thereupon; which he read in his place, and afterwards delivered in at the clerk's table, where the same were again twice read, and unanimously agreed to, one hundred and twelve members being present.

"For as much as all the endeavors of the united colonies, by the most decent representations and petitions to the king and parliament of Great Britain, to restore peace and security to America under the British government, and a reunion with that people, upon just and liberal terms, instead of a redress of grievances, have produced, from an imperious and vindictive administration, increased insult, oppression, and a vigorous attempt to effect our total destruction. By a late act, all these colonies are declared to be in rebellion, and out of the protection of the British crown, our properties subjected to confiscation, our people, when captivated, compelled to join in the plunder and murder of their relations and countrymen, and all former rapine and oppression of Americans declared legal and just. Fleets and armies are raised, and the aid of foreign troops engaged to assist these destructive purposes. The king's representa-

A Brief Inquiry into the True Nature and Character of Our Federal Government
by Abel P. Upshur (1840)

There is yet another view of this subject, which cannot be properly omitted. It has already been shown that, prior to the revolution, the colonies were separate and distinct, and were not, in any political sense, or for any purpose of government, "one people." The *sovereignty* over them was in the British crown; but that sovereignty was not *jointly over all*, but *separately over each*, and might have been abandoned as to some, and retained as to others. The declaration of independence broke this connection. By that act, and not by the subsequent recognition of their independence, the colonies became free States. What then became of the *sovereignty* of which we speak? It could not be in *abeyance*; the moment it was lost

---

tive in this colony hath not only withheld all the powers of government from operating for our safety, but, having retired on board an armed ship, is carrying on a piratical and savage war against us, tempting our slaves by every artifice to resort to him, and training and employing them against their masters.

"In this state of extreme danger, we have no alternative left, but an abject submission to the will of those overbearing tyrants, or a total separation from the crown and government of Great Britain, uniting and *exerting the strength of all America for defense*, and forming alliances with foreign powers for commerce and aid in war. Wherefore, appealing to the Searcher of all hearts for the sincerity of former declarations, expressing our desire to preserve our connection with that nation, and that we are driven from that inclination by their wicked councils, and the eternal laws of self-preservation; resolved, unanimously, that the delegates appointed to represent this colony in general congress, be instructed to propose to that respectable body, *to declare the united colonies free and independent states*, absolved from all allegiance to, or dependence upon the crown or parliament of Great Britain; and that they give the assent of this colony to that declaration, and to whatever measures may be thought proper and necessary by the congress, for forming foreign alliances, and a confederation of the colonies, at such time and in such manner as to them may seem best. Provided, that the power of forming government for, and the regulations of the internal concerns of each colony be left to the respective colonial legislatures.

"Resolved, unanimously, that a committee be appointed to prepare a declaration of rights, and such a plan of government, as will be most likely to maintain peace and order in this colony, and secure substantial and equal liberty to the people.

"And a committee was appointed of the following gentlemen: — Mr. Archibald Cary, Mr. Meriwether Smith, Mr. Mercer, Mr. Henry Lee, Mr. Treasurer, Mr. Henry, Mr. Dandridge, Mr. Edmund Randolph, Mr. Gilmer, Mr. Bland, Mr. Digges. Mr. Carrington, Mr. Thomas Ludwel Lee, Mr. Cabell, Mr. Jones, Mr. Blair, Mr. Fleming, Mr. Tazewell, Mr. Richard Cary, Mr. Bullit, Mr. Watts, Mr. Banister, Mr. Page, Mr. Starke, Mr. David Mason, Mr. Adams, Mr. Read and Mr. Thomas Lewis."

It is impossible to contemplate this proceeding on the part of Virginia, without being convinced that she acted from her own free and sovereign will; and that she, at least, did "presume" to establish a government for herself, without the least regard to "the recommendation or the pleasure of congress."

by the British crown it must have vested somewhere else. Doubtless it vested in the states themselves. But, as they were separate and distinct as colonies, the sovereignty over one could not vest, either in whole or in part, in any other. Each took to itself that sovereignty which applied to itself, and for which alone it had contended with the British crown, to wit, the sovereignty *over* itself. Thus each colony became a free and sovereign State. This is the character which they claim in the very terms of the declaration of independence; in this character they formed the colonial government, and in this character that government always regarded them. Indeed, even in the earlier treaties with foreign powers, the distinct sovereignty of the States is carefully recognized. Thus, the treaty of alliance with France, in 1778, is made between "the most Christian king and the United States of North America to wit: New Hampshire, Massachusetts Bay, Rhode Island, Connecticut," &c., enumerating them all by name. The same form is observed in the treaty of amity and commerce with the States General of the United Netherlands, in 1782, and in the treaty with Sweden, in 1783. In the convention with the Netherlands, in 1782, concerning recaptured vessels, the names of the States are *not* recited, but "the United States of America" is the style adopted; and so also in some others. This circumstance shows that the two forms of expression were considered equipollent; and that foreign nations, in treating with the revolutionary government, considered that they treated with distinct sovereignties, through their common agent, and not with a new nation, composed of all those sovereign countries together. It is true, they treated with them jointly, and not severally; they considered them all bound to the observance of their stipulations, and they believed that the common authority, which was established between and among them, was sufficient to secure that object. The provisional articles with Great Britain, in 1782, by which our independence was acknowledged, proceed upon the same idea. The first article declares, that "His Britannic Majesty acknowledges the said United States, *to wit*, New Hampshire, Massachusetts Bay, Rhode Island and Providence Plantations, Connecticut, New York, New Jersey, Pennsylvania, Delaware, Maryland, Virginia, North Carolina, South Carolina and Georgia, to be free, sovereign and independent States; that he treats with them as such," &c. Thus the very act, by which their former sovereign releases them from their allegiance to him, confirms to each one by name the sovereignty within its own limits, and acknowledges it to be a "free, sovereign, and independent State"; *united*, indeed, with all the others, but not as forming with them any new and separate nation. The language employed is not suited to convey any other idea. If it had been in the contemplation of the parties, that the States had merged themselves into a single nation, something like the following formula would naturally have suggested itself as proper. "His Britannic Majesty acknowledges that New Hampshire, Massachusetts Bay, &c., former colonies of Great Britain, and now united together as one people, are *a* free, sovereign and *independent state*," &c. The difference between the two forms of expression, and the strict adaptation of each to the state of things which it contemplates, will be apparent to every reader.

It requires strong and plain proof to authorize us to say, that a nation once sovereign has ceased to be so. And yet our author requires us to believe this of the colonies, although he acknowledges that he cannot tell, with any degree of confidence or precision, when, how, or to what extent the sovereignty, which they acquired by declaring their independence was surrendered. According to him, the colonies are to be *presumed* to have yielded this sovereignty to a government established by themselves for a special and temporary purpose, which existed only at their will, and by their aid and support; whose powers were wholly undefined, and for the most part, exercised by usurpation on its part, and legitimated only by the acquiescence of those who appointed it; whose authority was without any adequate sanction which it could itself apply, and which, as to all the important functions of sovereignty, was a mere name – the shadow of power without its substance! If the fact was really so, I venture to affirm that the history of the world affords no similar instance of folly and infatuation.

But, whatever may have been the condition of the colonies prior to 1781, there is no room for doubt on the subject, after the final ratification of the articles of confederation in that year. Those articles declare that "each State retains its sovereignty, freedom and independence, and every power, jurisdiction and right, which is not, by this confederation expressly delegated to the United States, in congress assembled." The obvious construction of this clause requires that we should apply these latter words, only to "powers, jurisdiction and rights"; some of which, as enjoyed by the States under the previous government, were clearly surrendered by the articles of confederation. But their *entire* sovereignty, their *entire* freedom, and their *entire* independence, are reserved, for these are not partible. Indeed, this is clear enough, from the provisions of that instrument, which, throughout, contemplate the States as free, sovereign and independent. It is singular, too, that it should escape the observation of any one, that the very fact of adopting those articles, and the course pursued in doing so, attest, with equal clearness and strength, the *previous* sovereignty and independence of the States. What had the States in their separate character to do with that act, if they formed altogether "one people"? And yet the States, and the States alone, performed it, each acting for itself, and binding itself. The articles were confirmed by ten States, as early as 1778, by another in 1779 and by another in 1780; and yet they were not obligatory until Maryland acceded to them, 1781. Nothing less than the ratification of them by *all* the States, each acting separately for itself, was deemed sufficient to give them any binding force or authority.

There is much force and meaning in the word "retains," as it occurs in the clause above quoted. Nothing can properly be said to be *retained*, which was not *possessed* before; and of course, the States possessed before "sovereignty, freedom and independence." These they retained without any qualification, or limitation, and they also retained every "power, jurisdiction and right," which they did not then *expressly* surrender.

If these views of the subject be not wholly deceptive, our author has hazarded, without due caution, the opinion that the colonies formed "one people," either before or after the declaration of independence; and that they are not to be regarded as sovereign States, after that event. For myself, I profess my utter inability to perceive, in their condition, any nearer approach to political personality or individuality, than may be found in a mere league or confederation between sovereign and independent states; and a very *loose* confederation theirs undoubtedly was.

{Chapter VI}

The third division of the work {(Judge Story's work)} commences with a history of the adoption of the constitution. This also is given in an abridged form; but it omits nothing which can be considered material to the inquiry. Perhaps the author has fallen into one error, an unimportant one, certainly, in stating that "at the time and place appointed, the representatives of twelve States assembled." When the deputies first met in Philadelphia, in May, 1787, the representatives of only *nine* States appeared; they were, soon after, joined by those of three others. The author next proceeds to state the various objections which were urged against the constitution, with the replies thereto; to examine the nature of that instrument; to ascertain whether it be a compact or not; to inquire who is the final judge or interpreter in constitutional controversies; to lay down rules of interpretation; and, finally, to examine the constitution in its several departments and separate clauses. In the execution of this part of his task, he has displayed great research, laborious industry, and extensive judicial learning. The brief summary which he has given of the arguments by which the constitution was assailed on the one hand, and defended on the other, is not only interesting as matter of history, but affords great aid in understanding that instrument. We should be careful, however, not to attach to these discussions an undue importance. All the members of the various conventions did not engage in the debates, and, of course, we have no means of determining by what process of reasoning they were led to their conclusions. And we cannot reasonably suppose that the debaters always expressed their deliberate and well weighed opinions in all the arguments, direct and collateral, by which they sought to achieve a single great purpose. We are not, therefore, to consider the constitution as the one thing or the other, merely because some of the framers, or some of the adopters of it, chose so to characterize it in their debates. Their arguments are valuable as guides to our judgments, but not as authority to bind them.

In the interpretation of the constitution, the author founds himself, whenever he can, upon the authority of the supreme court. This was to be expected; for, in so doing, he has, in most cases, only reiterated his own judicial decisions. We could not suppose that one, whose opinions are not lightly adopted, would advance, as a commentator, a principle which he rejected as a judge. In most cases, too, no higher authority in the interpretation of the constitution is known in our systems, and none *better* could be desired. It is only in questions of *political power*, involving the rights of the States in reference to the federal government, that any class of politicians are disposed to deny the authority of the judgments of the supreme court. We shall have occasion to examine this subject more at large, in a subsequent part of this review.

In discussing the various clauses of the constitution, the author displays great research, and a thorough acquaintance with the history of that instrument. It is not perceived, however, that he has presented any new views of it, or offered any new arguments in support of the constructions which it has heretofore received. As a compendium of what others have said and done upon the subject, his work is very valuable. It facilitates investigation, whilst, at the same time, it is so full of matter, as to render little farther investigation necessary. Even in this view of the subject, however, it would have been much more valuable if it had contained references to the authorities on which its various positions are founded, instead of merely extracting their substance. The reader who, with this book as his guide, undertakes to acquaint himself with the Constitution of the United States, must take the authority of the author as conclusive, in most cases; or else he will often find himself perplexed to discover the sources from which he derives his information. This is a great defect in a work of this sort, and is the less excusable, because it might have been easily avoided. A writer who undertakes to furnish a treatise upon a frame of government, in relation to which great and contested political questions have arisen, owes it alike to his reader and to himself, to name the sources whence he draws whatever information he ventures to impart, and the authorities upon which he founds whatever opinions he ventures to inculcate. The reader requires this for the satisfaction of his own judgment; and the writer ought to desire it as affording the best evidence of his own truth and candor.

In this division of the work, the author pursues the idea cautiously hinted in the first division, and more plainly announced in the second; and he now carries it boldly out in its results. Having informed us that, as colonies, we were "for many purposes one people," and that the declaration of independence made us "a nation *de facto*," he now assumes the broad ground that this "one people," or nation *de facto*, formed the constitution under which we live. The consequences of this position are very apparent throughout the remainder of the work. The inferences fairly deduced from it impart to the constitution its distinctive character, as the author understands it; and, of course, if this fundamental position be wrong, that instrument is not, in many of its provisions what he represents it to be. The reader, therefore, should settle this question for himself in the outset; because, if he differs from the author upon this point, he will be compelled to reject by far the most important part of the third and principal division of these commentaries.

The opinion, that the constitution was formed by "the people of the United States," as contradistinguished from the people of the several States, that is, as contradistinguished from the States as such, is founded exclusively on the particular terms of the preamble. The language is, "We, the people of the United States, do ordain and establish this constitution for the United States of America." "The people do ordain and establish, not contract and stipulate with each other. *The people of the United States*, not the distinct people of a particular State with the people of the other States." In thus relying on the language of the preamble, the author rejects the lights of history altogether. I will endeavor in the first place to meet him on his own ground.

It is an admitted rule, that the preamble of a statute may be resorted to in the construction of it; and it may, of course, be used to the same extent in the construction of a constitution, which is a supreme law. But the only purpose for which it can be used is to aid in the discovery of the true object and intention of the law, where these would otherwise be doubtful. The preamble can, in no case, be allowed to *contradict* the law, or to vary the meaning of its plain language. Still less can it be used *to change the true character of the lawmaking power*. If the preamble of the constitution had declared that it was made by the people of France or England, it might, indeed, have been received as evidence of that fact, in the absence of all proof to the contrary; but surely it would not be so received against the plain testimony of the instrument itself, and the authentic history of the transaction. If the convention which formed the Constitution was not, in point of fact, a convention of the people of the United States, it had no right to give itself that title; nor had it any right to act in that character, if it was appointed by a different power. And if the Constitution, when formed, was adopted by the several States, acting through their separate conventions, it is historically untrue that it was adopted by the aggregate people of the United States. The preamble, therefore, is of no sort of value in settling this question; and it is matter of just surprise that it should be so often referred to, and so pertinaciously relied on, for that purpose. History alone can settle all difficulties upon this subject.

The history of the preamble itself ought to have convinced our author, that the inference which he draws from it could not be allowed. On the 6th of August, 1787, the committee appointed for that purpose reported the first draft of a constitution. The preamble was in these words: "We, the people of the States of New Hampshire, Massachusetts, Rhode Island and Providence Plantations, Connecticut, New York, New Jersey, Pennsylvania, Delaware, Maryland, Virginia, North Carolina, South Carolina and Georgia, do ordain, declare and establish the following constitution, for the government of ourselves and our posterity." (1 Elliott's Debates, 255.) On the very next day this preamble was unanimously adopted; and the reader will at once perceive, that it carefully preserves the distinct sovereignty of the States, and discountenances all idea of consolidation. (*Ib.* 263.) The draft of the constitution thus submitted was discussed, and various alterations and amendments adopted, (but without any change in the preamble), until the 8th of September, 1787, when the following resolution was passed: "It was moved and seconded to appoint a committee of five, to revise the style of, and arrange the articles agreed to, by the house; which passed in the affirmative." (*Ib.* 324.) It is manifest that this committee had no power to change the *meaning* of anything which had been adopted, but were authorized merely to "revise the style," and arrange the matter in proper order. On the 12th of the same month they made their report. The preamble, as they reported it, is in the following words: "We, *the people of the United States*, in order to form a more perfect union, to establish justice, insure domestic tranquility, provide for the common defense, promote the general welfare, and secure the blessings of liberty to ourselves and our posterity, do ordain and establish this constitution for the United States of America." (*Ib.* 326.) It does not appear that any attempt was made to change this phraseology in any material point, or to reinstate the original. The presumption is, therefore, that the two were considered as substantially the same, particularly as the committee had no authority to make any change, except in the style. The difference in the mere phraseology of the two was certainly not overlooked; for on the 13th September, 1787, "it was moved and seconded to proceed to the comparing of the report from the committee of revision, with the articles which were agreed to by the house, and to them referred for arrangement; which passed in the affirmative. And the same was read by paragraphs, compared, and, in some places, corrected and amended." (*Ib.* 338.) In what particulars these corrections and amendments were made, we are not very distinctly informed. The only change which was made in the preamble, was by striking out the word "to," before the words "establish justice"; and the probability is, that no other change was made in any of the articles, except such as would make "the report of the committee of revision" "correspond with the articles agreed to by the house." The inference, therefore, is irresistible, that the convention considered the preamble reported by the committee of revision, as substantially corresponding with the original draft, as unanimously "agreed to by the house."

There is, however, another and a perfectly conclusive reason for the change of phraseology, from the States by name, to the more general expression "the United States"; and this, too, without supposing that it was intended thereby to convey a different idea as to the parties to the constitution. The revised draft contained a proviso, that the constitution should go into operation when adopted and ratified by *nine* States. It was, of course, uncertain whether more than nine would adopt it, or not, and if they should not, it would be altogether improper to name them as parties to that instrument. As to one of them, Rhode Island, she was not even represented in the convention, and, consequently, the others had no sort of right to insert her as a party. Hence it became necessary to adopt a form of expression which would apply to those who should ratify the constitution, and not to those who should refuse to do so. The expression actually adopted answers that purpose fully. It means simply, "We, the people of those States who have united for that purpose, do ordain," &c. This construction corresponds with the historical fact, and reconciles the language employed with the circumstances of the case. Indeed, similar language was not unusual, through the whole course of the revolution. "The people of his majesty's colonies," "the people of the united colonies," "the people of the United States," are forms of expression which frequently occur, without intending to convey any other idea than that of the people of the *several* colonies or States.

It is, perhaps, not altogether unworthy of remark, in reference to this inquiry, that the word "people" has no plural termination in our language. If it had, the probability is that the expression would have been "we, the peoples," conveying, distinctly, the idea of the people of the several States. But, as no such plural termination is known in our language, the least that we can say is, that the *want of it* affords no argument in favor of the author's position.

This brief history of the preamble, collected from the Journals of the Convention, will be sufficient to show that the author has allowed it an undue influence in his construction of the constitution. It is not from such vague and uncertain premises, that conclusions, so important and controlling, can be wisely drawn. The author, however, is perfectly consistent with himself in the two characters in which he appears before us; the *commentator* takes no ground which the *judge* does not furnish. It is remarkable that although this question was directly presented in the case of Martin *vs.* Hunter's Lessees, and although the fact, that the constitution of the United States "was ordained and established, not by the States in their sovereign capacities, but emphatically by the people of the United States," is made the foundation of the judgment of the supreme court in that case; yet, Judge Story, in delivering the opinion of the court, rests that position upon the preamble alone, and offers no other argument whatever to support it. And this too, although, in his own opinion, upon the right decision of that case rested "some of the most solid principles which have hitherto been supposed to sustain and protect the Constitution of the United States." It is much to be regretted, that principles so important should be advanced as mere dogmas, either by our judges, or by the instructors of our youth.

In this case, as in others, however, we ought not to be satisfied with simply proving that the author's conclusions are not warranted by the facts and arguments from which he derives them. Justice to the subject requires a much more full and detailed examination of this important and fundamental question.

I have endeavored to show, in the preceding part of this review, that the people of the several States, while in a colonial condition, were not "one people" in any political sense of the terms; that they did not become so by the declaration of independence, but that each State became a complete and perfect sovereignty within its own limits; that the revolutionary government, prior to the establishment of the confederation, was, emphatically, a government of the States as such, through congress, as their common agent and representative, and that, by the articles of confederation, each State expressly reserved its entire sovereignty and independence. In no one of the various conditions, through which we have hitherto traced them, do we perceive any feature of consolidation; but their character as distinct and sovereign States is always carefully and jealously preserved. We are, then, to contemplate them as sovereign States, when the first movements towards the formation of the present constitution were made.

Our author has given a correct history of the preparatory steps towards the call of a convention. It was one of those remarkable events, (of which the history of the world affords many examples), which have exerted the most important influence upon the destiny of mankind, and yet have sprung from causes which did not originally look to any such results. It is true, the defects of the confederation, and its total inadequacy to the purposes of an effective government, were generally acknowledged; but I am not aware that any decisive step was taken in any of the States, for the formation of a better system, prior to the year 1786. In that year, the difficulties and embarrassments under which our trade suffered, in consequence of the conflicting and often hostile commercial regulations of the several States, suggested to the legislature of Virginia the necessity of forming among all the States a general system, calculated to advance and protect the trade of all of them. They accordingly appointed commissioners, to meet at Annapolis commissioners from such of the other States as should approve of the proceeding, for the purpose of preparing a uniform plan of commercial regulations, which was to be submitted to all the States, and, if by them ratified and adopted, to be executed by congress. Such of the commissioners as met, however, soon discovered that the execution of the particular trust with which they were clothed, involved other subjects not within their commission, and which could not be properly adjusted without a great enlargement of their powers. They therefore simply reported this fact, and recommended to *their respective legislatures* to appoint delegates to meet in general convention in Philadelphia, for the purpose not merely of forming a uniform system of commercial regulations, but of reforming the government in any and every particular in which the interests of the States might require it. This report was also transmitted to congress, who approved of the recommendation it contained, and on the 21st of February, 1787, resolved, "that in the opinion of congress, it is expedient that, on the second Monday in May next, a convention of delegates who shall *have been appointed by the several States*, be held at Philadelphia, for the sole and express purpose of revising the articles of confederation, and reporting to congress and the *several legislatures*, such alterations and provisions therein, as shall, when agreed to in congress, and *confirmed by the States*, render the federal constitution adequate to the exigencies of government, and the preservation of the union." (1 Elliott's Debates, 155.)

Such was the origin of the convention of 1787. It is apparent that the delegates to that body were to be "appointed by the several States," and not by "the people of the United States"; that they were to report their proceedings to "congress and the several legislatures," and not to "the people of the United States"; and that their proceedings were to be part of the constitution, only when "agreed to in congress and confirmed by the States," and not when confirmed by "the people of the United States." Accordingly, delegates were, in point of fact, appointed by the States; those delegates did, in point of fact, report to congress and the States; and congress did, in point of fact, approve, and the States did, in point of fact, adopt, ratify and confirm the constitution which they formed. No other agency than that of the States as such, and of congress, which was strictly the representative of the States, is to be discerned in any part of this whole proceeding. We may well ask, therefore, from what unknown source our author derives the idea, that the constitution was formed by "the people of the United States," since the history of the transaction, even as he has himself detailed it, proves that "the people of the United States" did not appoint delegates to the convention, were not represented in that body, and did not adopt and confirm its act as their own!

Even, however, if the question now before us be not, merely and exclusively, a question of historical fact, there are other views of it scarcely less decisive against our author's position. In the first place, I have to remark, that *there were no such people* as "the people of the United States," in the sense in which he uses those terms. The articles of confederation formed, at that time, the only government of the United States; and, of course, we are to collect from them alone the true nature of the connection of the States with one another. Without deeming it necessary to enumerate all the powers which they conferred on congress, it is sufficient to remark that they were all exercised in the name of the States, as free, sovereign and independent States. Congress was, in the strictest sense, the representative of the States. The members were appointed by the States, in whatever mode each State might choose, without reference either to congress or the other States. They could, at their own will and pleasure, recall their representatives, and send others in their places, precisely as any sovereign may recall his minister at a foreign court. The members voted in congress by States, each State having one vote, whatever might be the number of its representatives. There was no president, or other common executive head. The States alone, as to all the more important operations of the government, were relied on to execute the resolves of congress. In all this, and in other features of the confederation which it is unnecessary to enumerate, we recognize a league between independent sovereignties, and not one nation composed of all of them together. It would seem to follow, as a necessary consequence, that if the States, thus united together by league, did not form one nation, there could not be a citizen or subject of that nation. Indeed, congress had *no power to make such citizen, either by naturalization or otherwise.* It is true, the citizens of every State were entitled, with certain exceptions, such as paupers, vagabonds, &c., to all the privileges of citizens of every other State, when within the territories thereof; but this was by express compact in the articles of confederation, and did not otherwise result from the nature of their political connection. It was only by virtue of citizenship in some particular State, that its citizens could enjoy within any other State the rights of citizens thereof. They were not known as *citizens of the United States*, in the legislation either of congress or of the several States. He who ceased to be a citizen of some particular State, without becoming a citizen of some other particular State, forfeited all the rights of a citizen in each and all of the States. There was no one right which the citizen could exercise, and no one duty which he could be called on to perform, except as a citizen of some particular State. In that character alone could he own real estate, vote at elections, sue or be sued; and in that character alone could he be called on to bear arms, or to pay taxes.

What, then, was this citizenship of the United States, which involved no allegiance, conferred no right and subjected to no duty? Who were "the people of the United States"? Where was their domicile, and what were the political relations, which they bore to one another? What was their sovereignty, and what was the nature of the allegiance which it claimed? Whenever these questions shall be satisfactorily answered without designating *the people of the several States, distinctively as such*, I shall feel myself in possession of new and unexpected lights upon the subject.

Even, however, if we concede that there was such a people as "the people of the United States," our author's position is still untenable. I admit that the people of any country may, if they choose, alter, amend or abrogate their form of government, or establish a new one, without invoking the aid of their constituted authorities. They *may* do this, simply because they have the physical power to do it, and not because such a proceeding would be either wise, just, or expedient. It would be *revolution* in the strictest sense of the term. Be this as it may, no one ever supposed that this course was pursued in the case under consideration. Every measure, both for the calling of the convention and for the ratification of the constitution, was adopted in strict conformity with the recommendations, resolutions and laws of congress and the State legislatures. And as "the people of the United States" *did not*, in point of fact, take the subject into their own hands, independent of the constituted authorities, they *could not* do it by any agency of those authorities. So far as the federal government was concerned, the articles of confederation, from which alone it derived its power, contained no provision by which "the people of the United States" could express authoritatively a joint and common purpose to change their government. A law of congress authorizing them to do so would have been void, for want of right in that body to pass it. No mode, which congress might have prescribed for ascertaining the will of the people upon the subject, could have had that sanction of legal authority, which would have been absolutely necessary to give it force and effect. It is equally clear that there was no right or power reserved to the States themselves, by virtue of which any such authoritative expression of the common will and purpose of the people of all the States could have been made. The power and jurisdiction of each state were limited to its own territory; it had no power to legislate for the people of any other State. No single State, therefore, could have effected such an object; and if they had all concurred in it, each acting, as it was only authorized to act, *for itself*, that would have been strictly the action of the *States as such*, and as contradistinguished from the action of the mass of the people of *all* the States. If "the people of the United States" could not, by any aid to be derived from their common government, have effected such a change in their constitution, that government itself was equally destitute of all power to do so. The only clause in the articles of confederation, touching this subject, is in the following words: "And the articles of this confederation shall be inviolably observed by every State, and the union shall be perpetual; nor shall any alteration, at any time hereafter, be made in any of them, unless such alteration be agreed to in congress of the United States, and *be afterwards confirmed by the legislature of every State*." Even if this power had been given to congress alone, without subjecting the exercise of it to the negative of the States, it would still have been the power of the States in their separate and independent capacities, and not the power of the people of the United States, as contradistinguished from them. For congress was, as we have already remarked, strictly the representative of the States; and each State, being entitled to one vote, and one only, was precisely equal, in the deliberations of that body, to each other State. Nothing less, therefore, than a *majority of the States*, could have carried the measure in question, even in congress. But, surely there can be no doubt that the power to change their common government was reserved to the States alone, when we see it expressly provided that nothing less than their *unanimous consent, as States*, should be sufficient to effect that object.

There is yet another view of this subject. It results from the nature of all government, freely and voluntarily established, that there is no power to *change*, except the power which *formed* it. It will scarcely be denied by any one, that the confederation was a government strictly of the States, formed by them as such, and deriving all its powers from their consent and agreement. What authority was there, *superior* to the States, which could undo their work? What power was there, other than that of the States themselves, which was authorized to declare that their solemn league and agreement should be abrogated? Could a majority of the people of all the States have done it? If so, whence did they derive that right? Certainly not from any agreement among the States, or the people of all the States; and it could not be legitimately derived from any other source. If, therefore, they had exercised such a power, it would have been a plain act of usurpation and violence. Besides, if we may judge from the apportionment of representation as proposed in the convention, a majority of the people of all the States were to be found in the four States of Massachusetts, New York, Pennsylvania and Virginia; so, that, upon this idea, the people of less than one-third of all the States could change the articles of confederation, although those articles expressly provided that they should not be changed without the consent of *all the States*! There was, then, no power superior to the power of the States; and, consequently, there was no power which could alter or abolish the government which they had established. If the Constitution has superseded the articles of confederation, it is because the parties to those articles have agreed that it should be so. If they have not so agreed, there is no such Constitution, and the articles of confederation are still the only political tie among the States. We need not, however, look beyond the attestation of the Constitution itself, for full evidence upon this point. It professes to have been "done by the unanimous consent of the States present, &c.," and not in the name or by the authority of "the people of the United States."

But it is not the mere *framing* of a constitution which gives it authority as such. It becomes obligatory only by its *adoption and ratification*; and surely that act, I speak of free and voluntary government, makes it the constitution of those only who do adopt it. Let us ascertain then, from the authentic history of the times, by whom our own constitution was adopted and ratified.

The resolution of congress already quoted, contemplates a convention "for the sole and express purpose of revising the articles of confederation," and reporting suitable "alterations and provisions therein." The proceedings of the convention were to be reported to congress and the several legislatures, and were to become obligatory, only when "agreed to in congress and confirmed by the States." This is precisely the course of proceeding prescribed in the articles of confederation. Accordingly, the new constitution was submitted to congress; was by them approved and agreed to, and was afterwards, in pursuance of the recommendation of the convention, laid before conventions of the several States, and by them ratified and adopted. In this proceeding, each State acted for itself, without reference to any other State. They ratified at different periods; some of them unconditionally, and others with provisos and propositions for amendment. This was certainly *State action*, in as distinct a form as can well be imagined. Indeed, it may well be doubted whether any other form of ratification, than by the States themselves would have been valid. At all events, none other was contemplated, since the Constitution itself provides, that it shall become obligatory, when ratified by "nine States," between the States ratifying the same. "The people of the United States," as an aggregate mass, are nowhere appealed to, for authority and sanction to that instrument. Even if they could have made it their constitution, by adopting it, they could not, being as they were separate and distinct political communities, have united themselves into one mass for that purpose, without previously overthrowing their own municipal governments; and, even then, the new constitution would have been obligatory only on those who agreed to and adopted it, and not on the rest.

The distinction between the people of the several States and the people of the United States, as it is to be understood in reference to the present subject, is perfectly plain. I have already explained the terms "a people," when used in a political sense. The distinction of which I speak may be illustrated by a single example. If the Constitution had been made by "the people of the United States," a certain portion of those people would have had authority to adopt it. In the absence of all express provision to the contrary, we may concede that a *majority* would, *prima facie*, have had that right. Did that majority, in fact, adopt it? Was it ever ascertained whether a majority of the *whole people* were in favor of it or not? Was there any provision, either of law or constitution, by which it was possible to ascertain that fact? It is perfectly well known that there was no such provision; that no such majority was ever ascertained, or even contemplated. Let us suppose that the people of the States of Massachusetts, New York, Pennsylvania and Virginia, containing, as we have seen they probably did, a majority of the whole people, had been unanimous against the Constitution, and that a bare majority of the people in each of the other nine States, acting in their separate character as States, had adopted and ratified it. There can be no doubt, that it would have become the constitution of the United States; and that, too, by the suffrages of a decided minority, probably not exceeding one-fourth of the aggregate people of all the States. This single example shows, conclusively, that the people of the United States, as contradistinguished from the people of the several States, had nothing to do, and could not have had anything to do with the matter.

This brief history of the formation and adoption of the constitution, which is familiar to the mind of everyone who has attended to the subject at all, ought, as it seems to me, to be perfectly satisfactory and conclusive; and should silence forever, all those arguments in favor of consolidation, which are founded on the preamble to that instrument. I do not perceive with what propriety it can be said, that the "people of the United States," formed the Constitution, since they neither appointed the convention, nor ratified their act, nor otherwise adopted it as obligatory upon them. Even if the preamble be entitled to all the influence which has been allowed to it, our author's construction of its language is not, as has already been remarked, the only one of which it is susceptible. "We, the people of the United States," may, without any violence to the rules of fair construction, mean "we, the people of the States united." In this acceptation, its terms conform to the history of the preamble itself, to that of the whole Constitution, and those who made it. In any other acceptation, they are either without meaning, or else they affirm what history proves to be false.

It would not, perhaps, have been deemed necessary to bestow quite so much attention on this part of the work, if it were not evident that the author himself considered it of great consequence, not as matter of history, but as warranting and controlling his construction of the Constitution, in some of its most important provisions. The argument is not yet exhausted, and I am aware that much of what I have said is trite, and that little, perhaps no part of it, is new. Indeed, the subject has been so often and so ably discussed, particularly in parliamentary debates, that it admits very few new views, and still fewer new arguments in support of old views. It is still, however, an open question, and there is nothing in the present condition of public opinion, to deprive it of any portion of its original importance. The idea that the people of these States were, while colonists, and, consequently, are now, "one people," in some sense which has never been explained, and to some extent which has never been defined, is constantly inculcated by those who are anxious to consolidate all the powers of the States in the federal government. It is remarkable, however, that scarcely one systematic argument, and very few attempts of any sort, have yet been made to *prove* this important position. Even the vast and clear mind of the late chief justice of the United States, which never failed to disembarrass and elucidate the most obscure and intricate subject, appears to have shrunk from this. In all his judicial opinions in which the question has been presented, the unity or identity of the people of the United States has been taken as a postulate, without one serious attempt to prove it. The continued repetition of this idea, and the boldness with which it is advanced, have, I am induced to think, given it an undue credit with the public. Few men, far too few, inquire narrowly into the subject, and even those who do, are not in general skeptical enough to doubt what is so often and so peremptorily asserted; and asserted, too, with

A Brief Inquiry into the True Nature and Character of Our Federal Government
by Abel P. Upshur (1840)

that sort of hardy confidence which seems to say, that all argument to prove it true would be supererogatory and useless. It is not, therefore, out of place, nor out of time, to refresh the memory of the reader, in regard to those well-established historical facts, which are sufficient in themselves, to prove that the foundation on which the consolidationists build their theory is unsubstantial and fallacious.

I would not be understood as contending, in what I have already said, that the constitution is *necessarily* federative, *merely* because it was made by the States as such, and not by the aggregate people of the United States. I readily admit, that although the previous system was strictly federative, and *could* not have been changed except by the States who made it, yet there was nothing to prevent the States from surrendering, in the provisions of the new system which they adopted, all their power, and even their separate existence, if they chose to do so. The true inquiry is, therefore, whether they have in fact done so, or not; or, in other words, what is the true character, in this respect, of the present Constitution. In this inquiry, the history of their previous condition, and of the Constitution itself, is highly influential and important.

The author, carrying out the idea of a unity between the people of the United States, which, in the previous part of his work, he had treated as a postulate, very naturally, and indeed necessarily, concludes that the Constitution is not a *compact* among sovereign States. He contends that it is "not a contract imposing mutual obligations, and contemplating the permanent subsistence of parties having an independent right to construe, control and judge of its obligations. If in this latter sense, it is to be deemed a compact, it must be, either because it contains, on its face, stipulations to that effect, or because it is necessarily implied, from the nature and objects of a frame of government."

There is a want of appositeness and accuracy in the first sentence of this extract, which renders it somewhat difficult to determine whether the author designed it as a single proposition, or as a series of independent propositions. If the first, there is not one person in the

United States, it is presumed, who would venture to differ from him. I confess, however, that I do not very clearly discern what bearing it has on the question he was examining. It involves no point of difference between political parties, nor does it propound any question which has heretofore been contested, or which may be expected to arise hereafter, touching the true nature of the Constitution. If he designed a series of propositions, then the two first are so obviously false, that the author himself would not venture to maintain them, and the last is so obviously true, that no one would dream of denying it. For example. He can scarcely mean to say that our government is not a "contract," whether made by the States as such, or by "the people of the United States"; and it is perfectly clear that it "contemplates the permanent subsistence of the parties to it," whoever those parties may be. These two propositions, therefore, taken distinctly, are not true in themselves, and neither of them was necessary, as qualifying or forming a part of the third. And, as to the third, it is not easy to see why he announced it, since it never entered into the conception of any one, that the parties to the Constitution had "an independent right," as a general right, "to construe, *control* or judge of its obligations." We all admit that the power and authority of the federal government, within its constitutional sphere, are superior to those of the States, in some instances, and co-ordinate in others, and that every citizen is under an absolute obligation to render them respect and obedience; and this *simply because his own State, by the act of ratifying the Constitution, has commanded him to do so*. We all admit it to be true, as a general proposition, that no citizen nor State has an independent right to "construe," and still less to "control," the constitutional obligations of that government, and that neither a citizen nor a State can "judge," that is, *decide*, on the nature and extent of those obligations, with a view to control them. All that has ever been contended for is, that a State has a right to judge of its *own* obligations, and, consequently, to judge of those of the federal government, so far as they relate to *such State itself*, and no farther. It is admitted on all hands, that when the *federal government transcends its constitutional power*, and when, of course, it is not acting *within* its "obligations," the parties to that government, whoever they may be, are no longer under any duty to respect or obey it. This has been repeatedly affirmed by our courts, both State and federal, and has never been denied by any class of politicians. Who then is to determine, whether it has so transcended its constitutional obligations or not? It is admitted that to a certain extent the supreme court is the proper tribunal in the last resort, because the States, in establishing that tribunal, have expressly agreed to make it so. The jurisdiction of the federal courts extends to certain cases, affecting the rights of the individual citizens, and to certain others affecting those of the individual States. So far as the federal government is authorized to act on the individual citizen, the powers of the one and the rights of the other, are properly determinable by the federal courts. And the decision is binding too, and absolutely final, so far as the relation of the citizen to the *federal government* is concerned. There is not, within that system, any tribunal of appeal, from the decisions of the supreme court. And so also of those cases in which the rights of *the States* are referred to the federal tribunals. In this sense, and to this extent, it is strictly true that the parties have not "an independent right to construe, control and judge, of the obligations" of the federal government, but they are bound by the decisions of the federal courts, so far as they have authorized and agreed to submit to them. But there are many cases involving the question of federal power which are not cognizable before the federal courts; and, of course, as to these, we must look out for some other umpire. It is precisely in this case that the question, who are the parties to the constitution, becomes all important and controlling. If the States are parties as sovereign States, then it follows, as a necessary consequence, that each of them has the right which belongs to every sovereignty, to construe its own contracts and agreements, and to decide upon its own rights and powers. I shall take occasion, in a subsequent part of this review, to enter more fully into the question, who is the common umpire. The statement here given, of the leading point of difference between the great political parties of the country, is designed only to show that the author's proposition does not involve it. That proposition may mislead the judgment of the reader, but cannot possibly enlighten it, in regard to the true nature of the Constitution.

He has been scarcely less unfortunate in the next proposition. Taking his words in their most enlarged sense, he is probably correct in his idea, though he is not accurate in his language; but in the sense in which his own reasoning shows that he himself understands them, his proposition is wholly untenable. If, by the words "stipulations to that effect," he means simply that the effect must necessarily result from the provisions of the Constitution, he has merely asserted a truism which no one will dispute with him. Certainly, if it does not result from the nature of all government, that it is a compact, and if there be nothing in our Constitution to show that *it* is so, then it is *not* a compact. His own reasoning, however, shows that he means by the word "stipulations," something in the nature of *express* agreement or declaration; and, in that sense, the proposition is obviously untrue, and altogether defective as a statement for argument. It is very possible that our Constitution may be a compact, even though it contain no express agreement or declaration so denominating it, and though it may not "result from the nature and objects of *a* frame of government," that it is so; and this simply because it may "result from the nature and objects of *our* government" that it is a compact, whether such be the result of *other* governments or not. If the author designed to take this view of the subject, the examination which he has given of the Constitution, in reference to it, is scarcely as extended and philosophical as we had a right to expect from him. He has not even alluded to the frame and structure of the government in its several departments, nor presented any such analysis of it in any respect, as to enable the reader to form any satisfactory conclusion as to its true character in the particular under consideration. Everything which he has urged as argument to prove his proposition, may well be true, and every sentence of the Constitution, which he has cited for that purpose, may be allowed its full effect, and yet our government may be a compact, even in the strictest sense in which he has understood the term.

His first argument is, that the "United States were no strangers to compacts of this nature," and that those who ratified the Constitution, if they had meant it as a compact, would have used "appropriate *terms*" to convey that idea. I have already shown that if he means by this, that the Constitution would have contained some express declaration to that effect, he is altogether inaccurate. He himself knows, as a *judge*, that a deed, or other instrument, receives its distinctive character, not from the *name* which the parties may choose to give to it, but from its *legal effect and operation*. The same rule applies to constitutions. Ours is a compact or not, precisely as its provisions make it so, or otherwise. The question, who are the parties to it, may influence, and ought to influence, the construction of it in this respect; and I propose presently to show, from this and other views of it, that it is, in its nature, "a mere confederation," and not a consolidated government, in any one respect. It *does*, therefore, contain "appropriate terms," if we take those words in an enlarged sense, to convey the idea of a compact.

Our author supposes, however, that a "conclusive" argument upon this subject is furnished by that clause of the Constitution which declares that "This Constitution, and the laws of the United States, which shall be made in pursuance thereof, and all treaties made, or which shall be made, under the authority of the United States, shall be the supreme law of the land; and the judges in every State, shall be bound thereby, anything in the constitution or laws of any State to the contrary notwithstanding." Hence he concludes that "the people of any State cannot, by any form of its own constitution or laws, or other proceedings, repeal, or abrogate or suspend it."

Here again the author displays a want of proper definiteness and precision, in the statement of his proposition. The people who *make* a law, can, upon the principles of all our institutions, either "repeal or abrogate or suspend it"; and if, as he supposes, our constitution was made by "the people of the United States," in the aggregate, then "the people of any State," or of half a State, may repeal, or abrogate, or suspend it, if they happen to be a majority of the whole. The argument, therefore, if we are to take it in the full latitude in which it is laid down, is not sound, upon the author's own principles; and it can avail nothing, except upon the very supposition which he disallows; to wit, that the Constitution was formed by the States, and not by the people of the United States. Even in this acceptation, however, I am at a loss to perceive how it establishes the proposition with which he set out; to wit, that the Constitution is not a compact. Certainly it is very possible so to frame a compact, that no party to it shall have a right either to "repeal or abrogate or suspend it"; and if it be possible to do so, then the mere absence of such right does not even *tend* to disprove the existence of compact. Our own Constitution, even in the opinion of those who are supposed by the author to be least friendly to it, is a compact of precisely this nature. The Nullifier contends only for the right of a State to *prevent the Constitution from being violated by the general government*, and not for the right either to repeal, abrogate or suspend it. The Seceder asserts only that a State is competent to withdraw from the Union whenever it pleases; but does not assert that in so doing it can repeal, or abrogate or suspend the Constitution, as to the other States. Secession would, indeed, utterly destroy the compact as to the seceding party; but would not necessarily affect its obligation as to the rest. If it would, then the rest would have no right to coerce the seceding State, nor to place her in the attitude of an enemy. It is certain, I think, they would *not* have such right; but those who assert that they would – and the author is among the number – must either abandon that idea, or they must admit that the act of secession does not break up the Constitution, except as to the seceding State. For the moment the Constitution is destroyed, all the authorities which it has established cease to exist. There is no longer such a government as that of the United States, and, of course, they cannot, as such, either make any demand, or assert any right, or enforce any claim.

The conclusion, however, to which our author has arrived, upon this point, is not that to which he originally designed that his premises should conduct him. The question of the right of a party to a compact, to repeal or abrogate or suspend it, does not enter into his original proposition, nor result from the argument which he had immediately before used to sustain it. The proposition is, that our Constitution is not a compact, and the argument is, that it is not a compact, because it is a supreme law. The same idea is substantially reaffirmed, in the next argument by which he proposes to prove the main proposition. "The design" (of the Constitution) "is to establish a government. This, of itself, imports legal obligation, permanence, and uncontrollability by any, but the authorities authorized to alter or abolish it."

Admitting, as I cheerfully do, that all this is strictly true, I am yet unable to perceive how it demonstrates that our Constitution is not a compact. May not a compact between sovereign States, be a government? Is there any such necessary restraint upon, or incident of, sovereign power, that it cannot, in any possible exercise of it, produce such a result? If there is, then it was incumbent on the author to show it, because, if there is not, his argument is of no force; and he himself will admit, that the proposition, to say the least of it, is not quite clear enough to be taken as a postulate. His own historical information, if he had drawn on its ample funds, must have furnished him with numerous instances of governments established by compact. He need, not, however, have gone beyond our own Confederation, which, although a compact among sovereign States, in the strictest sense, was yet treated as a government by the people at home, and recognized as such by all foreign powers. It was also "supreme," within its prescribed sphere of action; its rights and powers over the most important subjects of general concern were not only superior to those of the States, but were *exclusive*. The author's proposition and argument, reduced to their simple terms, may be thus stated. "Our Constitution is not a compact, because it is a government, and because that government is the supreme law." There are few minds, I think, prepared to embrace this conclusion, or to discern the connection which it has with the premises. There are still fewer who will not feel surprise, that our *author* should have formed such a conclusion, since an instance to disprove it, furnished by the history of his own country, and existing in his own times, had but just passed under his critical examination and review.

The remaining arguments upon this point are merely inferences drawn from the absence of *express* words in the Constitution, or from the opinions of members of the various conventions, expressed in the debates concerning it. These have already been sufficiently examined. Taking his whole chapter upon this subject together, the reader will probably think that it does not answer the expectations which the public have formed upon the author's powers as a reasoner. His political opponents will be apt to think, also, that he has done something less than justice to them, in the view which he has given of their principles. After laboring, in the way we have seen, to prove that our Constitution is not a compact, he informs us that "The cardinal conclusion for which this doctrine of a compact has been, with so much ingenuity and ability, forced into the language of the Constitution, (for the latter nowhere alludes to it), is avowedly to establish that, in construing the Constitution, there is no common umpire; but that, each State, nay, each department of the government of each State, is the supreme judge for itself, of the powers and rights and duties arising under that instrument."

The author must excuse me – I mean no disrespect to him – if I express my unfeigned astonishment that he should have admitted this passage into a grave and deliberate work on the Constitution. He must, indeed, have been a most careless observer of passing events, and a still more careless reader of the publications of the last ten years, upon this very point, if he has found either in the one or the other, the slightest authority for the opinion which is here advanced. The most ultra of those who have contended for the rights of the States have asserted no such doctrine as he has imputed to them. Neither is it the necessary or legitimate consequence of any principle which they have avowed. I cannot impute to an author of his acknowledged ability, the weakness of stating a proposition merely for the sake of the poor triumph of refuting it. With what other motive, then, did he make a statement which is unsupported, as matter of fact; which involves no disputed or *doubted* question of constitutional law, and which attributes to a large class of his fellow-citizens opinions which would justly expose them to the scorn of all correct thinkers? That class profess to hold, in their utmost latitude and in their strictest applications, the doctrines of the State Rights' school of politics. They believe that those doctrines contain the only principle truly conservative of our Constitution; that without them there is no effective check upon the federal government, and, of course, that that government can increase its own powers to an indefinite extent; that this must happen in the natural course of events, and that, ultimately, the whole character of our government will be so changed, that even its *forms* will be rejected, as cumbrous and useless, under the monarchy, in substance, into which we shall have insensibly glided. It is, therefore, because they are lovers of the Constitution and of the Union, that they contend strenuously for the rights of the States. They are no lovers of anarchy nor of revolution. Their principles will cease to be dear to them, whenever they shall cease to subserve the purposes of good order, and of regular and established government. It is their object to preserve the institutions of the country as they are, sincerely believing that nothing more than this is necessary to secure to the people all the blessings which can be expected from any government whatever. They would consider themselves but little entitled to respect as a political party, if they maintained the loose, disjointed, and worse than puerile notions, which the author has not thought it unbecoming to impute to them.

It is the peculiar misfortune of the political party to which I have alluded, to be misunderstood and misrepresented in their doctrines. The passage above quoted affords not the least striking instance of this. It is a great mistake to suppose that they have ever contended that the right of State interposition was given in the express terms of the Constitution; and, therefore, they have *not* "forced this principle into the language of that instrument. The right in question is supposed to belong to the States, only because *it is an incident of their sovereignty, which the Constitution has not taken away*. The author, it is presumed, could scarcely have failed to perceive the difference of the two propositions, nor could he have been unconscious that they did not depend upon the same course of investigation or reasoning. And it is not true, so far as my information extends, that any political party has ever asserted, *as a general proposition*, that, in construing the Constitution, there is no common umpire. Cases have already been stated, in which the supreme court is universally admitted to be the common umpire, and others will be stated when we come more directly to that part of our subject. In the broad sense, then, in which the author lays down the proposition, it has never been contended for by any political party whatever. Neither is it true, as he is pleased to assert, that any political party has ever supposed, that "each department of the government of each State" had a right to "judge for itself, of the powers, rights and duties, arising under" the Constitution. By the word "judge," he must be understood to mean *decide finally*; and, in this sense, I venture to affirm that no political party, nor political partizan, even in the wildest dream of political frenzy, has ever entertained the absurd notion here attributed to them. It is difficult to suppose that the author could have been uninformed of the fact, that nothing short of the power of all the State, acting through its own constituted authorities, has ever been deemed of the least force in this matter. The better and more prevalent opinion is, that a State cannot properly so act, except by a convention called for that express purpose. This was the course pursued by South Carolina; but in the case of the alien and sedition laws, Virginia acted through her ordinary legislature. As to this matter, however, the legislature was very properly considered as representing the power of the *whole* State.

Thus, in the short paragraph above quoted, the author has fallen into three most remarkable errors, proving that he has, in the strangest way imaginable, misunderstood the principles which he attempted to explain. The young and plastic minds to which he addressed himself, with the professed object of instructing them in the *truths* of constitutional interpretation, will look in vain for the publication or other authority which sustains him. And the political party whose principles he has endeavored to hold up to reproach, has a right to demand of him, why he has chosen to attribute to them absurd and revolutionary notions, unworthy alike of their patriotism and their reason.

It is submitted to the reader's judgment to determine how far the reasoning of the author, which we have just examined, supports his position that our Constitution is not a compact. The opinion of that congress which recommended the call of the convention seems to have been very different; they, at least, did not suppose that a compact could not be a government. Their resolution recommends the call of a convention, for the purpose of "revising the articles of confederation, and reporting such alterations and provisions *therein*, as would render the *federal constitution* adequate to the exigencies of government, and the preservation of the Union." In the opinion of congress, the articles of confederation, which were clearly a compact, were an *inadequate* constitution, and therefore, they recommended such alterations and provisions *therein*, as would make that same compact an *adequate* constitution. Nothing is said about forming a new government, or changing the essential character of the existing one; and, in fact, no such thing was contemplated at the time. "The sole and exclusive purpose" of the convention was so to amend, or add to, the provisions of the articles of confederation, as would form "a more perfect union, &c.," upon the principles of the union already existing. It is clear, therefore, that, in the opinion of congress, and of all the States that adopted their recommendation, that union or compact was a constitution of government

It is worthy of remark, that of the States, New Hampshire and the author's own State of Massachusetts, expressly call the Constitution a compact, in their acts of ratification; and no other State indicates a different view of it. This tends to prove that public opinion at the time had not drawn the nice distinction which is now insisted on, between a government and a compact; and that those who for eight years had been living under a compact, and forming treaties with foreign powers by virtue of its provisions, had never for a moment imagined that it was not a government.

But little importance, however, ought to be attached to reasoning of this kind. Those who contend that our Constitution is a compact, very properly place their principles upon much higher ground. They say that the Constitution is a compact, *because it was made by sovereign States, and because that is the only mode in which sovereign States treat with one another*. The conclusion follows irresistibly from the premises; and those who would deny the one, are bound to disprove the other. Our adversaries *begin* to reason at the very point at which reasoning becomes no longer necessary. Instead of disproving our premises, they *assume* that they are wrong, and then triumphantly deny our conclusion also. If we establish that the Constitution was made by the States, and that they were, at the time, distinct, independent and perfect sovereignties, it follows that they could not treat with one another, even with *a view* to the formation of a new common government, except in their several and sovereign characters. They must have maintained the same character when they entered upon that work, and throughout the whole progress of it. Whatever the government may be, therefore, in its essential character, whether a federative or a consolidative government, it is still a compact, or the result of a compact, because those who made it *could not* make it in any other way. In determining its essential character, therefore, we are bound to regard it as a compact, and to give it such a construction as is consistent with that idea. We are not to *presume* that the parties to it designed to change the character in which they negotiated with one another. Every fair and legitimate inference is otherwise. Its sovereignty is the very last thing which a nation is willing to surrender; and nothing short of the clearest proof can warrant us in concluding that it has surrendered it. In all cases, therefore, where the language and spirit of the Constitution are doubtful, and even where their most natural construction would be in favor of consolidation, (if there be any such case), we should still incline against it, and in favor of the rights of the States, unless no other construction can be admitted.

{Chapter VII}

Having disposed of this preliminary question, we now approach the Constitution itself. I affirm that it is, in its structure, a federative and not a consolidated government; that it is so, in all its departments, and in all its leading and distinguishing provisions; and, of course, that it is to be so interpreted, *by the force of its own terms*, apart from any influence to be derived from that rule of construction which has just been laid down. We will first examine it in the structure of its several departments.

The Legislature. – This consists of two houses. The senate is composed of two members from each State, chosen by its own legislature, whatever be its size or population, and is universally admitted to be strictly federative in its structure. The house of representatives consists of members chosen in each State, and is regulated in its numbers, according to a prescribed ratio of representation. The number to which each State is entitled is proportioned to its own population, and not to the population of the United States; and if there happen to be a surplus in any State less than the established ratio, that surplus is not added to the surplus or population of any other State, in order to make up the requisite number for a representative, but is wholly unrepresented. In the choice of representatives, each State votes by itself, and for its own representatives, and not in connection with any other State, nor for the representatives of any other State. Each State prescribes the qualifications of its own voters, the Constitution only providing that they shall have the qualifications which such State may have prescribed for the voters for the most numerous branch of its own legislature. And, as the *right* to vote is prescribed by the State, the *duty* of doing so cannot be enforced, except by the authority of the State. No one can be elected to represent any State, except a citizen thereof. Vacancies in the representation of any State, are to be supplied under writs of election, issued by the executive of such State. In all this, there is not one feature of nationality. The whole arrangement has reference to the States as such, and is carried into effect solely by their authority. The federal government has no agency in the choice of representatives, except only that it may prescribe the "times, places and manner, of holding elections." It can neither prescribe the qualifications of the electors, nor impose any penalty upon them, for refusing to elect. The States alone can do these things; and, of course, the very existence of the house of representatives depends, as much as does that of the senate, upon the action of the States. A State may withdraw its representation altogether, and congress has no power to prevent it, nor to supply the vacancy thus created. If the house of representatives were national, in any practical sense of the term, the "nation" would have authority to provide for the appointment of its members, to prescribe the qualifications of voters, and to enforce the performance of that duty. All these things the State legislatures can do, within their respective States, and it is obvious that they are strictly national. In order to make the house of representatives equally so, the people of the United States must be so consolidated that the federal government may distribute them, without regard to State boundaries, into numbers according to the prescribed ratio; so that *all* the people may be represented, and no unrepresented surplus be left in any State. If these things could be done under the Federal Constitution, there would then be a strict analogy between the popular branches of the federal and State legislatures, and the former might, with propriety, be considered "national." But it is difficult to imagine a national legislature which does not exist under the authority of the nation, and over the very appointment of which the nation, as such, can exert no effective control.

There are only two reasons which I have ever heard assigned for the opinion that the house of representatives is national, and not federative. The first is, that its measures are carried by the votes of a majority of the *whole number*, and not by those of a majority of the States. It would be easy to demonstrate that this fact does not warrant such a conclusion; but all reasoning is unnecessary, since the conclusion is disproved by the example of the other branch of the federal legislature. The senate, which is strictly federative, votes in the same way. The argument, therefore, proves nothing, because it proves too much.

The second argument is, that the States are not *equally* represented, but each one has a representation proportioned to its population. There is no reason, apparent to me, why a league may not be formed among independent sovereignties, giving to each an influence in the management of their common concerns, proportioned to its strength, its wealth, or the interest which it has at stake. This is but simple justice, and the rule ought to prevail in all cases, except where higher considerations disallow it. History abounds with examples of such confederations, one of which I will cite. The States General of the United Provinces were strictly a federal body. The council of state had almost exclusively the management and control of all their military and financial concerns; and in that body, Holland and some other provinces had three votes each, whilst some had two, and others only one vote each. Yet it never was supposed that for this reason the United Provinces were a consolidated nation. A single example of this sort affords a full illustration of the subject, and renders all farther argument superfluous.

It is not, however, from the apportionment of its powers, nor from the modes in which those powers are exercised, that we can determine the true character of a legislative body, in the particular now under consideration. The true rule of decision is found in the manner in which the body is constituted, and that, we have already seen, is, in the case before us, federative, and not national.

We may safely admit, however, that the house of representatives is not federative, and yet contend, with perfect security, that *the legislative department* is so. Congress consists of the house of representatives and senate. Neither is a complete legislature, in itself, and neither can pass any law without the concurrence of the other. And, as the senate is the peculiar representative of the States, no act of legislation whatever can be performed, without the consent of the States. They hold, therefore, a complete check and control over the powers of the people in this respect, even admitting that those powers are truly and strictly represented in the other branch. It is true that the check is mutual; but if the legislative department were national, there would be no federative feature in it. It cannot be replied, with equal propriety, that, if it were federative, there would be no national feature in it. The question is, whether or not the States have preserved their distinct sovereign characters, in this feature of the Constitution. If they have done so, in any part of it, the whole must be considered federative; because national legislation implies a *unity*, which is absolutely inconsistent with all idea of a confederation; whereas, there is nothing to prevent the members of a confederation from exerting their several powers, in any form of *joint action* which may seem to them proper.

But there is one other provision of the Constitution which appears to me to be altogether decisive upon this point. Each State, whatever be its population, is entitled to at least one representative. It may so happen that the unrepresented surplus, in some one State, may be greater than the whole population of some other State; and yet such latter State would be entitled to a representative. Upon what principle is this? Surely, if the house of representatives were national, something like *equality* would be found in the constitution of it. Large surpluses would not be arbitrarily rejected in some places, and smaller numbers, not equal to the general ratio, be represented in others. There can be but one reason for this: As the Constitution was made by the States, the true principles of the confederation could not be preserved, without giving to each party to the compact a place and influence in each branch of the common legislature. This was due to their perfect *equality* as sovereign States.

The Executive. – In the election of the president and vice president, the exclusive agency of the States, as such, is preserved with equal distinctness. These officers are chosen by electors, who are themselves chosen by the people of each State, acting by and for itself, and in such mode as itself may prescribe. The number of electors to which each State is entitled is equal to the whole number of its representatives *and senators*. This provision is even more federative than that which apportions representation in the house of representatives; because it adds two to the electors of each State, and, so far, places them upon an equality, whatever be their comparative population. The people of each State vote *within* the State, and not elsewhere; and for their own electors, and for no others. Each State prescribes the qualifications of its own electors, and can alone compel them to vote. The electors, when chosen, give their votes within their respective States, and at such times and places as the States may respectively prescribe.

There is not the least trace of national agency, in any part of this proceeding. The federal government can exercise no rightful power in the choice of its own executive. "The people of the United States" are equally unseen in that important measure. Neither a majority, nor the whole of them together, can choose a president, except in their character of citizens of the several States. Nay, a president may be constitutionally elected, *with a decided majority of the people against him*. For example, New York has forty-two votes, Pennsylvania thirty, Virginia twenty-three, Ohio twenty-one, North Carolina fifteen, Kentucky fourteen, and South Carolina fifteen. These seven States can give a majority of all the votes, and each may elect its own electors by a majority of only one vote. If we add their minorities to the votes of the other States, (supposing those States to be unanimous against the candidate), we may have a president constitutionally elected, with less than half – perhaps with little more than a fourth – of the people in his favor. It is true that he may also be constitutionally elected, with the majority of the *States*, as such against him, as the above example shows; because the States may, as before remarked, properly agree, by the provisions of their compact, that they shall possess influence, in this respect, proportioned to their population. But there is no mode, consistent with the true principles of free, representative government, by which a minority of those to whom *en masse*, the elective franchise is confided can countervail the concurrent and opposing action of the majority. If the president could be chosen by the people of "the United States" in the aggregate, instead of by the States, it is difficult to imagine a case in which a majority of those people, concurring in the same vote, could be overbalanced by a minority.

All doubt upon this point, however, is removed by another provision of the Constitution touching this subject. If no candidate should receive a majority of votes in the electoral colleges, the house of representatives elects the president, from the three candidates who have received the largest electoral vote. In doing this two-thirds of the States must be present by their representatives, or one of them, and then *they vote by States, all the members from each State giving one vote, and a majority of all the States being necessary to a choice.* This is precisely the rule which prevailed in the ordinary legislation of that body, under the articles of confederation, and which proved its federative character, as strongly as any other provision of those articles. Why, then, should this federative principle be preserved, in the election of the president by the house of representatives, if it was designed to abandon it, in the election of the same officer by the electoral colleges? No good reason for it has yet been assigned, so far as I am informed. On the contrary, there is every just reason to suppose, that those who considered the principle safe and necessary in one form of election, would adhere to it as equally safe and necessary in every other, with respect to the same public trust. And this is still farther proved by the provision of the Constitution relating to the election of the *vice* president. In case of the death or constitutional disability of the president, every executive trust devolves on him; and, of course, the same general principle should be applied, in the election of both of them. This is done in express terms, so far as the action of the electoral colleges is contemplated. But if those colleges should fail to elect a vice president, that trust devolves on the *senate*, who are to choose from the two highest candidates. Here the federative principle is distinctly seen; for the senate is the representative of the States.

This view of the subject is still farther confirmed by the clause of the Constitution relating to impeachments. The power to try the president is vested in the senate alone, that is, in the representatives of the States. There is a strict fitness and propriety in this; for those only, whose officer the president is, should be entrusted with the power to remove him.

It is believed to be neither a forced nor an unreasonable conclusion from all this, that the executive department is, in its structure, strictly federative.

The Judiciary. – The judges are nominated by the president, and approved by the senate. Thus the nominations are made by a federative officer, and the approval and confirmation of them depend on those who are the exclusive representatives of the States. This agency is manifestly federative, and "the people of the United States" cannot mingle in it, in any form whatever.

As the Constitution is federative in the structure of all three of its great departments, it is equally so *in the power of amendment.*

Congress may *propose* amendments, "whenever two-thirds of both houses shall deem it necessary." This secures the States against any action upon the subject, by the people at large. In like manner, congress may call a convention for proposing amendments, "on the application of the legislatures of two-thirds of the several States." It is remarkable that, whether congress or the States act upon the subject, the *same proportion* is required; not less than two-thirds of either being authorized to act. From this it is not unreasonable to conclude, that the convention considered that the *same power* would act in both cases; to wit, the power of the States, who might effect their object either by their separate action as States, or by the action of congress, their common federative agent; but, whether they adopted the one mode or the other, not less than two-thirds of them should be authorized to act efficiently.

The amendments thus proposed "shall be valid to all intents and purposes, as part of this Constitution, *when ratified by the legislatures of three-fourths of the several States, or by conventions in three-fourths thereof,* as the one or the other mode of ratification may be proposed by congress." It is the act of adoption or ratification alone which makes a constitution. In the case before us, the States alone can perform that act. The language of the Constitution admits of no doubt, and gives no pretext for double construction. It is not the people of the United States in the aggregate, merely *acting* in their several States, who can ratify amendments. *Three-fourths of the several States* can alone do this. The idea of separate and independent political corporations could not be more distinctly conveyed, by any form of words. If the people of the United States, as one people, but acting in their several States, could ratify amendments, then the very language of the Constitution requires that *three-fourths of them* shall concur therein. Is it not, then, truly wonderful that no mode has yet been prescribed to ascertain whether three-fourths of them do concur or not? By what power can the necessary arrangement upon this point be effected? In point of fact, amendments have already been made, in strict conformity with this provision of the Constitution. We ask our author, whether three-fourths of the people of the United States concurred in those amendments or not; and if they did, whence does he derive the proof of it?

If our author, and the politicians of his school, be correct in the idea, that the Constitution was formed by "the people of the United States," and not by the States, as such, this clause relating to amendments presents a singular anomaly in politics. Their idea is, that the State sovereignties were merged, to a certain extent, in that act, and that the government established was emphatically the government of the people of the United States. And yet, those same people can neither alter nor amend that government! In order to perform this essential function, it is necessary to call again into life and action those very State sovereignties which were supposed to be merged and dead, by the very act of *creating* the instrument which they are required to amend! To alter or amend a government requires the same extent of power which is required to *form* one; for every alteration or amendment is, as to so much, a new government. And, of all political acts, the formation of a constitution of government is that which admits and implies, the most distinctly and to the fullest extent, the existence of absolute, unqualified, unconditional and unlimited sovereignty. So long, therefore, as the power of amending the Constitution rests exclusively with the States, it is idle to contend that they are less sovereign now than they were before the adoption of that instrument.

A Brief Inquiry into the True Nature and Character of Our Federal Government
by Abel P. Upshur (1840)

The idea which I am endeavoring to enforce, of the federative character of the Constitution, is still farther confirmed by that clause of the article under consideration, which provides that no amendment shall be made to deprive any State of its equal suffrage in the senate, without its own consent. So strongly were the States attached to that perfect equality which their perfect sovereignty implied, and so jealous were they of every attack upon it, that they guarded it, by an express provision of the Constitution, against the possibility of overthrow. All other rights they confided to that power of amendment which they reposed in three-fourths of all the States; but *this* they refused to entrust, except to the separate, independent and sovereign will of each State; giving to each, in its own case, an absolute negative upon all the rest.[*]

The object of the preceding pages has been to show that the Constitution is federative, in the power which framed it; federative in the power which adopted and ratified it; federative in the power which sustains and keeps it alive; federative in the power by which alone it can be altered or amended; and federative in the structure of all its departments. In what respect, then, can it justly be called a consolidated or national government? Certainly, the mere fact that, in particular cases, it is authorized to act directly on the people, does not disprove its federative character, since that very sovereignty in the States, which a confederation implies, includes within it the right of the State to subject its own citizens to the action of the common authority of the confederated States, in any form which may seem proper to itself. Neither is our Constitution to be deemed the less federative, because it was the object of those who formed it to establish "a government," and one effective for all the legitimate purposes of government. Much emphasis has been laid upon this word, and it has even been thought, by one distinguished statesman of Judge Story's school, that ours is "*a government proper*," which I presume implies

---

[*] So absolutely is the federal government dependent on the States for its existence at all times, that it may be absolutely dissolved, without the least violence, by the simple refusal of a part of the States to act. If, for example, a few States, having a majority of electoral votes, should refuse to appoint electors of president and vice-president, there would be no constitutional executive, and the whole machinery of the government would stop.

that it is a government in a peculiarly emphatic sense. I confess that I do not very clearly discern the difference between a government and a government proper. Nothing is a government which is not *properly* so; and whatever is properly a government, is a government proper. But whether ours is a "government proper," or only a simple government, does not prove that it is not a confederation, unless it be true that a confederation cannot be a government. For myself, I am unable to discover why States, absolutely sovereign, may not create for themselves, by compact, a common government, with powers as extensive and supreme as any sovereign people can confer on a government established by themselves. In what other particular ours is a consolidated or national government, I leave it to the advocates of that doctrine to show.

{Chapter VIII}

We come now to a more particular and detailed examination of the question, "Who is the final judge or interpreter in constitutional controversies?" The fourth chapter of this division of the author's work is devoted to this inquiry; and the elaborate examination which he has given to the subject, shows that he attached a just importance to it. The conclusion, however, to which he has arrived, leaves still unsettled the most difficult and contested propositions which belong to this part of the Constitution. His conclusion is, that, "in all questions of a judicial nature," the supreme court of the United States is the final umpire; and that the *States*, as well as individuals, are absolutely bound by its decisions. His reasoning upon this part of the subject is not new, and does not strike me as being particularly forcible. Without deeming it necessary to follow him in the precise order of his argument, I shall endeavor to meet it in all its parts, in the progress of this examination. Its general outline is this: It is within the proper function of the judiciary to interpret the laws; the Constitution is the supreme law, and therefore it is within the proper function of the judiciary to interpret the Constitution; of course, it is the province of the federal judiciary to interpret the Federal Constitution. And as that Constitution, and all laws made in pursuance thereof, are the supreme law of the land, anything in the laws or constitution of any State to the contrary notwithstanding, therefore, the interpretations of that Constitution, as given by the supreme court, are obligatory, final and conclusive, upon the people and the States.

Before we enter upon this investigation, it is proper to place the proposition to be discussed in terms somewhat more definite and precise than those which the author has employed. What, then, is meant by "final judge and interpreter"? In the ordinary acceptation of these terms, we should understand by them a tribunal having lawful cognizance of a subject, and from whose decisions there is no appeal. In this view of the question there can be no difficulty in admitting that the decisions of the supreme court are final and conclusive. Whatever comes within the legitimate cognizance of that tribunal, it has a right to decide, whether it be a question of the law, or of the Constitution; and no other tribunal can reverse its decision. The Constitution, which creates the supreme court, creates no other court of superior or appellate jurisdiction to it; and, consequently, its decisions are strictly "final." There is no power *in the same government to which that court belongs*, to reverse or control it, nor are there any means *therein* of resisting its authority. So far, therefore, as the *Federal Constitution* has provided for the subject at all, the supreme court is, beyond question, the final judge or arbiter; and this, too, whether the jurisdiction which it exercises be legitimate or usurped.

The terms "constitutional controversies" are still more indefinite. Every controversy which is submitted to the decision of a judicial tribunal, whether State or Federal, necessarily involves the constitutionality of the law under which it arises. If the law be not constitutional, the court cannot enforce it, and, of course, the question whether it be constitutional or not, necessarily arises in every case to which the court is asked to apply it. The very act of enforcing a law presupposes that its constitutionality has been determined. In this sense, every court, whether State or federal, is the "judge or arbiter of constitutional controversies," arising in causes before it; and if there be no appeal from its decision, it is the "final" judge or arbiter, in the sense already expressed.

Let us now inquire *what* "constitutional controversies" the federal courts have authority to decide, and how far its decisions are final and conclusive against all the world.

The third article of the Constitution provides that "The judicial powers shall extend to all cases in law and equity, arising under this Constitution, the laws of the United States, and the treaties made, or which shall be made, under their authority; to all cases affecting ambassadors, other public ministers and consuls; to all cases of admiralty and maritime jurisdiction; to controversies to which the United States shall be a party; to controversies between two or more States; between a State and citizens of another State; between citizens of different States; between citizens of the same State, claiming lands, under grants of different States; and between a State and the citizens thereof, and foreign States, citizens or subjects."

The eleventh amendment provides that "The judicial power of the United States shall not be construed to extend to any suit in law or equity, commenced or prosecuted against one of the United States, by citizens of another State, or by citizens or subjects of any foreign State."

It will be conceded on all hands that the federal courts have no jurisdiction except what is here conferred. The judiciary, as a part of the federal government, derives its powers only from the Constitution which creates that government. The term "cases" implies that the subject matter shall be proper for judicial decision; and the *parties* between whom alone jurisdiction can be entertained, are specifically enumerated. Beyond these "cases" and these parties they have no jurisdiction.

There is no part of the Constitution in which the framers of it have displayed a more jealous care of the rights of the States, than in the limitations of the judicial power. It is remarkable that no power is conferred except what is absolutely necessary to carry into effect the general design, and accomplish the general object of the States, as independent, confederated States. The federal tribunals cannot take cognizance of any case whatever in which all the States have not an equal and common interest that a just and impartial decision shall be had. A brief analysis of the provisions of the Constitution, will make this sufficiently clear.

Cases "arising under the Constitution" are those in which some right or privilege is denied, which the Constitution confers, or something is done, which the Constitution prohibits, as expressed in the Constitution itself. Those which arise "under the laws of the United States" are such as involve rights or duties, which result from the legislation of congress. Cases of these kinds are simply the carrying out of the compact or agreement made between the States, by the Constitution itself, and, of course, all the States are alike interested in them. For this reason alone, if there were no other, they ought to be entrusted to the common tribunals of all the States. There is another reason, however, equally conclusive. The judicial should always be at least co-extensive with the legislative power; for it would be a strange anomaly, and could produce nothing but disorder and confusion, to confer on a government the power to *make* a law, without conferring, at the same time, the right to interpret, and the power to enforce it.

Cases arising under treaties, made under the authority of the United States, and those "affecting ambassadors and other public ministers and consuls," could not properly be entrusted to any other than the federal tribunals. Treaties are made under the common authority of all the States, and all, alike, are bound for the faithful observance of them. Ambassadors and other public ministers and consuls are received under the common authority of all the States, and their duties relate only to matters involving alike the interests of all. The peace of the country, and the harmony of its relations with foreign powers, depend, in a peculiar degree, on the good faith with which its duties in reference to these subjects are discharged. Hence it would be unsafe to entrust them to any other than their own control; and even if this were not so, it would be altogether incongruous to appeal to a State tribunal, to enforce the rights, the obligations or the duties of the United States. For like reasons, cases of admiralty and maritime jurisdiction are properly entrusted to the federal tribunals.

Controversies to which the United States shall be a party should, upon general principles, belong only to her own courts. There would be neither propriety nor justice in permitting any one State to decide a case in which all the States are parties. In like manner those between two or more States – between a State and citizens of another State, where the State is plaintiff – (it cannot *be sued*) – and between citizens of different States, could not be entrusted to the tribunals of any particular State interested, or whose citizens are interested therein, without danger of injustice and partiality. Jurisdiction is given to the federal courts, in these cases, simply because they are equally interested for all the parties, are the common courts of all the parties, and therefore are presumed to form the only fair and impartial tribunal between them. The same reasoning applies to cases between citizens of the same State, claiming lands under grants of different States. Cases of this sort involve questions of the sovereign power of the States, and could not, with any show of propriety, be entrusted to the decision of either of them, interested as it would be to sustain its own acts, against those of the sister State. The jurisdiction in this case is given upon the same principles which give it in cases between two or more States.

Controversies between a State or the citizens thereof, and foreign States, citizens or subjects, depend on a different principle, but one equally affecting the common rights and interests of all the States. A foreign State cannot, of course, be sued; she can appear in our courts only as plaintiff. Yet, in whatever form such controversies, or those affecting the citizens of a foreign State, may arise, all the States have a deep interest that an impartial tribunal, satisfactory to the foreign party, should be provided. The denial of justice is a legitimate, and not an unfruitful cause of war. As no State can be involved in war without involving all the rest, they all have a common interest to withdraw from the State tribunals a jurisdiction which may bring them within the danger of that result. All the States are alike bound to render justice to foreign States and their people; and this common responsibility gives them a right to demand that every question involving it shall be decided by their common judicatory.

This brief review of the judicial power of the United States, as given in the Constitution, is not offered as a full analysis of the subject; for the question before us does not render any such analysis necessary. My design has been only to show with what extreme reserve judicial power has been conferred, and with what caution it has been restricted to those cases, only, which the new relation between the States, established by the Constitution, rendered absolutely necessary. In all the cases above supposed, the jurisdiction of the federal courts is clear and undoubted; and as the States have, in the frame of the Constitution, agreed to submit to the exercise of this jurisdiction, they are bound to do so, and to compel their people to like submission. But it is to be remarked, that they are bound only *by* their agreement, and not *beyond* it. They are under no obligation to submit to the decisions of the supreme court, on subject matter not properly cognizable before it, nor to those between parties not responsible to its jurisdiction. Who, then, is to decide this point? Shall the supreme court decide it for itself, and against all the world? It is admitted that every court must necessarily determine every question of jurisdiction which arises before it, and, so far, it must of course be the judge of its own powers. If it be a court of the last resort, its decision is necessarily final, so far as those authorities are concerned, which belong to the same system of government with itself. There is, in fact, no absolute and certain limitation, in any constitutional government, to the powers of its own judiciary; for, as those powers are derived from the Constitution, and as the judges are the interpreters of the Constitution, there is nothing to prevent them from interpreting in favor of any power which they may claim. The supreme court, therefore, *may* assume jurisdiction over subjects and between parties, not allowed by the constitution, and there is no power in the *federal government* to gainsay it. Even the impeachment and removal of the judges, for ignorance or corruption, would not invalidate their decisions already pronounced. Is there, then, no redress? The Constitution itself will answer this question, in the most satisfactory manner.

The tenth article of the amendments of the Constitution provides that "The powers not delegated to the United States by the Constitution, nor prohibited by it to the States, are reserved to the States respectively, or to the people." The powers thus reserved, are not only reserved against the federal government in whole, but against each and every department thereof. The judiciary is no more excepted out of the reservation than is the legislature or the executive. Of what nature, then, are those reserved powers? Not the powers, if any such there be, which are possessed by all the States together, for the reservation is to "the States *respectively*"; that is, to each State separately and distinctly. Now we can form no idea of any power possessed by a State as such, and independent of every other State, which is not, in its nature, a sovereign power. Every power so reserved, therefore, must be of such a character that each State may exercise it, without the least reference or responsibility to any other State whatever.

We have already seen that the Constitution of the United States was formed by the States *as such*, and the reservation above quoted is an admission that, in performing that work, they acted as independent and sovereign States. It is incident to every sovereignty to be alone the judge of its own compacts and agreements. No other State or assemblage of States has the least right to interfere with it, in this respect, and cannot do so without impairing its sovereignty. The Constitution of the United States is but the agreement which each State has made, with each and all the other States, and is not distinguishable, in the principle we are examining, from any other agreement between sovereign States. Each State, therefore, has a right to interpret that agreement for itself, unless it has clearly waived that right in favor of another power. That the right is not waived in the case under consideration, is apparent from the fact already stated, that if the judiciary be the sole judges of the extent of their own powers, their powers are universal, and the enumeration in the Constitution is idle and useless. But it is still farther apparent from the following view.

The Federal Government is the creature of the States. It is not a party to the Constitution, but the result of it – the creation of that agreement which was made by the States as parties. It is a mere agent, entrusted with limited powers for certain specific objects; which powers and objects are enumerated in the Constitution. Shall the agent be permitted to judge of the extent of his own powers, without reference to his constituent? To a certain extent he is compelled to do this, in the very act of exercising them, but this is always in subordination to the authority by whom his powers were conferred. If this were not so, the result would be, that the agent would possess every power which the constituent could confer, notwithstanding the plainest and most express terms of the grant. This would be against all principle and all reason. If such a rule should prevail in regard to government, a written constitution would be the idlest thing imaginable. It would afford no barrier against the usurpations of the government, and no security for the rights and liberties of the people. If then the *federal government* has no authority to judge, in the last resort, of the extent of its own powers, with what propriety can it be said that *a single department* of that government may do so? Nay, it is said that this department may not only judge for itself, but for the other departments also. This is an absurdity as pernicious as it is gross and palpable. If the judiciary may determine the powers of the federal government, it may pronounce them either less or more than they really are. That government at least would have no right to complain of the decisions of an umpire which it had chosen for itself, and endeavored to force upon the States and the people. Thus a single department might deny to both the others, salutary powers which they really possessed, and which the public interest or the public safety might require them to exercise; or it might confer on them powers never conceded, inconsistent with private right, and dangerous to public liberty.

In construing the powers of a free and equal government, it is enough to disprove the existence of any rule, to show that such consequences as these will result from it. Nothing short of the plainest and most unequivocal language should reconcile us to the adoption of such a rule. No such language can be found in our Constitution. The only clause, from which the rule can be supposed to be derived, is that which confers jurisdiction in "all cases arising under the Constitution, and the laws made in pursuance thereof"; but this clause is clearly not susceptible of any such construction. Every right may be said to be a constitutional right, because no right exists which the Constitution disallows; and consequently every remedy to enforce those rights presents "a case arising under the Constitution." But a construction so latitudinous will scarcely be contended for by anyone. The clause under consideration gives jurisdiction only as to those matters, and between those parties, enumerated in the Constitution itself. Whenever such a case arises, the federal courts have cognizance of it; but the right to decide a case arising *under* the Constitution does not necessarily imply the right to determine *in the last resort* what that Constitution is. If the federal courts should, in the very teeth of the eleventh amendment, take jurisdiction of cases "commenced or prosecuted against one of the States by citizens of another State," the decision of those courts, that they *had* jurisdiction, would certainly not settle the Constitution in that particular. The State would be under no obligation to submit to such a decision, and it would resist it by virtue of its sovereign right to decide for itself, whether it had agreed to the exercise of such a jurisdiction or not.

Considering the nature of our system of government, the States ought to be, and I presume always will be, extremely careful not to interpose their sovereign power against the decisions of the supreme court in any case where that court clearly has jurisdiction. Of this character are the cases already cited at the commencement of this inquiry; such, for example, as those between two States, those affecting foreign ministers, those of admiralty and maritime jurisdiction, &c. As to all these subjects the jurisdiction is clear, and no State can have any interest to dispute it. The decisions of the supreme court, therefore, ought to be considered as final and conclusive, and it would be a breach of the contract on the part of any State to refuse submission to them. There are, however, many cases involving questions of the powers of government, State and federal, which cannot assume a proper form for judicial investigation. Most questions of mere political power, are of this sort; and such are all questions between a State and the United States. As to these, the Constitution confers no jurisdiction on the federal courts, and, of course, it provides no common umpire to whose decision they can be referred. In such cases, therefore, the State must of necessity decide for itself. But there are also cases between citizen and citizen, arising under the laws of the United States, and between the United States and the citizen, arising in the same way. So far as the federal tribunals have cognizance of such cases, their decisions are final. If the constitutionality of the law under which the case arises, should come into question, the court has *authority* to decide it, and there is no relief for the parties, in any other judicial proceeding. If the decision, in a controversy between the United States and a citizen, should be against the United States, it is, of course, final and conclusive. If the decision should be against the citizen, his only relief is by an appeal to his own State. He is under no obligation to submit to federal decisions at all, except so far only as his own State has commanded him to do so; and he has, therefore, a perfect right to ask his State whether her commands extend to the particular case or not. He does not ask whether the federal court has *interpreted the law* correctly or not, but whether or not she *ever consented that congress should pass the law*. If congress had such power, he has no relief, for the decision of the highest federal court is final; if congress had not such power, then he is oppressed by the action of a usurped authority, and has a right to look to his own State for redress. His State may interpose in his favor or not, as she may think proper. If she does not, then there is an end of the matter; if she does, then it is no longer a judicial question. The question is then between new parties, who are not bound by the former decision; between a sovereign State and its own agent; between a State and the United States. As between these parties the federal tribunals have no jurisdiction, there is no longer a common umpire to whom the controversy can be referred. The State must of necessity judge for itself, by virtue of that inherent, sovereign power and authority, which, as to this matter, it has never surrendered to any other tribunal. Its decision, whatever it may be, is binding upon itself and upon its own people, and no farther.

A great variety of cases are possible, some of which are not unlikely to arise, involving the true construction of the Federal Constitution, but which could not possibly be presented to the courts, in a form proper for their decision. The following are examples.

By the 4th section of the 4th article it is provided that "Congress shall guaranty to every State in the Union a republican form of government." What is a republican form of government, and how shall the question be decided? In its very nature, it is a political, and not a judicial question, and it is not easy to imagine by what contrivance it could be brought before a court. Suppose a State should adopt a constitution not republican, in the opinion of congress; what course would be pursued? Congress might, by resolution, determine that the Constitution was not republican, and direct the State to form a new one. And suppose that the State should refuse to do so, on the ground that it had already complied with the requisitions of the Federal Constitution in that respect? Could congress direct an issue to try the question at the bar of the supreme court? This would, indeed, be an odd way of settling the rights of nations, and determining the extent of their powers! Besides, who would be parties to the issue; at whose suit should the State be summoned to appear and answer? Not at that of the United States, because a State cannot be sued by the United States, in a federal court; not at that of any other State, nor of any individual citizen, because they are not concerned in the question. It is obvious that the case does not present proper subject matter for judicial investigation; and even if it did, that no parties could be found authorized to present the issue.

Again, congress has authority "to provide for organizing, arming and disciplining the militia, and for governing such part of them as may be employed in the service of the United States; reserving to the States, respectively, the appointment of the officers, and the authority of training the militia according to the discipline prescribed by congress." Suppose that congress should usurp the right to appoint the militia officers, or the State should insist on training the militia in their own way, and not "according to the discipline prescribed by congress." How could this matter be brought before the supreme court? and even if properly brought there, how could its sentence be executed?

Again, suppose that congress should enact that all the slaves of the country should immediately be free. This is certainly not *impossible*, and I fear not even *improbable*, although it would be the grossest and most palpable violation of the constitutional rights of the slaveholder. This would certainly produce the most direct conflict between the State and Federal governments. It would involve a mere question of political power – the question whether the act of congress forbidding slavery, or the laws and constitution of the State allowing it, should prevail. And yet it is manifest that it presents no subject matter proper for judicial decision, and that the parties to it could not be convened before the supreme court.

These examples are sufficient to show that there is a large class of "constitutional controversies," which could not possibly be brought under the cognizance of *any* judicial tribunal, and still less under that of the federal courts. As to these cases, therefore, each State must of necessity, for the reasons already stated, be its own "final judge or interpreter." They involve the mere question of political power, as between the State and federal governments; and the fact, that they are clearly withheld from the jurisdiction of the supreme court, goes far to prove that the States in framing the Constitution did not design to submit to that court any question of the like kind, in whatever form or between whatever parties it might arise, except so far only as the parties themselves were concerned.

Our author himself does not contend that the supreme court is the "final judge or interpreter" in all cases whatsoever; he, of course, admits that no court can decide any question which is not susceptible of a proper form for judicial inquiry. But he contends that, in all cases of which the supreme court can take cognizance, its decisions are final, and absolutely binding and conclusive in all respects, to all purposes, and against the States and their people. It is this sweeping conclusion which it has been my object to disprove. I can see in the federal courts nothing more than the ordinary functions of the judiciary in every country. It is their proper province to interpret the laws; but their decisions are not binding, except between the parties litigant and their privies. So far as they may claim the force of *authority*, they are not *conclusive*, even upon those who pronounce them, and certainly are not so beyond the sphere of their own government. Although the judiciary may, and frequently do, enlarge or contract the powers of their own governments, as generally understood, yet they can never enlarge or contract those of *other* governments, for the simple reason, that other governments are not bound by their decisions. And so in our own systems. There is no case in which a judicial question can arise, before a federal court, between a State and the federal government. Upon what principle, then, are the States bound by the decisions of the federal judiciary? Upon no principle, certainly, except that, as to certain subjects, they have agreed to be so bound. But this agreement they made in their character of sovereign States, not with the federal government, but with one another. As sovereign States they alone are to determine the nature and extent of that agreement, and, of course, they alone are to determine whether or not they have given the federal courts authority to bind them in any given case. This principle has frequently been asserted by the States, and always successfully.*

But these mere technical rules, upon which we have hitherto considered the subject, are altogether unworthy of its importance, and far beneath its dignity. Sovereign nations do not ask their judges what are their rights, nor do they limit their powers by judicial precedents. Still less do they entrust these important subjects to judicial tribunals not their own, and, least of all, to the tribunals of that power against which their own power is asserted. It would have been a gross inconsistency in the States of our Union to do this, since they have shown, in every part of their compact with one another, the most jealous care of their separate sovereignty and independence. It is true they have agreed to be bound by the decisions of federal tribunals in certain specified cases, and it is not to be doubted that, so long as they desire the continuance of their present union, they will *feel* themselves bound, in every case which comes plainly within their agreement. There is no necessity to call in the aid of the supreme court to ascertain to what subjects, and how far, that agreement extends. So far as it is plain, it will be strictly observed, as national faith and honor require; there is no other guarantee. So far as it is not plain, or so far as it may be the will and pleasure of any State to deny or to resist it, the utter impotency of courts of justice to settle the difficulty will be manifested beyond all doubt. They will be admonished of their responsibility to the

---

* Hunter and Martin, *Cohen* vs. *State of Virginia*, and other cases.

power which created them. *The States* created them. They are but an emanation of the sovereign power of the States, and can neither limit nor control that power.

Ordinarily, the judiciary are the proper interpreters of the powers of government, but they interpret in subordination to the power which created them. In governments established by an aggregate people, such as are those of the States, a proper corrective is always found in the people themselves. If the judicial interpretation confer too much or too little power on the government, a ready remedy is found in an amendment of the Constitution. But in our federal system the evil is without remedy, if the federal courts be allowed to fix the limits of federal power with reference to those of the States. It would place everything in the State governments, except their mere existence, at the mercy of a single department of the federal government. The maxim, *stare decisis*, is not always adhered to by our courts; their own decisions are not held to be absolutely binding upon themselves. They may establish a right today and unsettle it tomorrow. A decision of the supreme court might arrest a State in the full exercise of an important and necessary power, which a previous decision of the same court had ascertained that she possessed. Thus the powers of the State governments, as to many important objects, might be kept indeterminate and constantly liable to change, so that they would lose their efficiency, and forfeit all title to confidence and respect. It is true, that in this case, too, there is a *possible* corrective in the power to amend the Constitution. But that power is not with the aggrieved State alone; it could be exerted only in connection with other States, whose aid she might not be able to command. And even if she could command it, the process would be too slow to afford effectual relief. It is impossible to imagine that any free and sovereign State ever designed to surrender her power of self-protection in a case like this, or ever meant to authorize any other power to reduce her to a situation so helpless and contemptible.*

---

* This want of uniformity and fixedness, in the decisions of courts, renders the supreme court the most unfit umpire that could be selected, between the federal government and the States, on questions involving their respective rights and powers. Suppose that the United States should resolve to cut a canal through the territory of Virginia; and being resisted, the

Yielding, therefore, to the supreme court all the jurisdiction and authority which properly belongs to it, we cannot safely or wisely repose in it the vast trust of ascertaining, defining or limiting the sovereign powers of the States.

Let us now follow the author in the inquiry, by what rules shall the Constitution be interpreted? Many of those which he has given are merely such as we apply to every instrument, and they do not, therefore, require any particular examination. The principal one, and that from which he deduces many others as consequences, is this: "It is to be construed as a frame or fundamental law of government, established by the people of the United States, according to their own free pleasure and sovereign will. In this respect, it is in no wise distinguishable from the constitutions of the State governments." That our Constitution is "a frame of government" will scarcely be denied by any one, and this, whether it be in its nature federative or consolidated. It is also, as is every other constitution of government, "a fundamental law." It is the acknowledged basis of all federal power and authority, the sole chart by which federal officers are to direct their course. But all this leaves the inquiry still open, what *is* this fundamental law, what is the course indicated by this chart of federal power, and how is it to be ascertained? The author seems to suppose that a full answer to this question may be found in the fact, that this frame or fundamental law of government was established by "the people of the United States, according to their

---

supreme court should decide that they had a right to do so. Suppose that, when the work was completed, a similar attempt should be made in Massachusetts; and being resisted, the same court should decide that they had *no* right to do so. The effect would be that the United States would possess a right in one State, which it did not possess in another. Suppose that Virginia should impose a tax on the arsenals, dock-yards, &c. of the United States within her territory, and that, in a suit to determine the right, the supreme court should decide in favor of it. Suppose that a like attempt should be made by Massachusetts, and, upon a similar appeal to that court, it should decide *against* it; Virginia would enjoy a right in reference to the United States, which would be denied to Massachusetts. Other cases may be supposed, involving like consequences, and showing the absurdity of submitting to courts of justice the decision of controversies between governments, involving the extent and nature of their powers.

I know that the decisions of the supreme court on constitutional questions have been very consistent and uniform; but that affords no proof that they will be so through all time to come. It is enough for the purposes of the present argument, that they *may* be otherwise.

free pleasure and sovereign will." If the fact were really so, it would undoubtedly exert an important influence, and would go far to justify his construction of the Constitution. We here discern the usefulness and necessity of that historical inquiry, which has just been finished. From that inquiry we learn, distinctly and without doubt, that the Constitution was *not* established by "the people of the United States," and consequently, that it does *not* resemble in that respect the constitutions of the States. There is no such analogy between them, as will presently be shown, as to require that they should be construed by the same rules. *The Constitution of the United States is to be considered as a compact or confederation between free, independent and sovereign States, and is to be construed as such, in all cases where its language is doubtful.* This is the leading and fundamental rule, from which the following may be deduced as consequences.

It is to be construed *strictly*. Our author supposes that the Constitution of the United States ought to "receive as favorable a construction as those of the States"; that it is to be liberally construed; that doubtful words are to be taken most strongly in *favor* of the powers of the federal government; and that there is "no solid objection to implied powers." All these are but inferences from the great rule which he first laid down, to wit, that the Constitution is to be considered as a frame of government, established by the people of the United States. As that rule cannot apply, because the fact on which it is founded is not true, it would seem to follow, as a necessary consequence, that the inferences deduced from it cannot be allowed. Nevertheless, they shall receive a more particular consideration under the present inquiry.

According to the principles of all our institutions, sovereignty does not reside in any government whatever, neither State nor federal. Government is regarded merely as the agent of those who create it, and subject in all respects to their will. In the States, the sovereign power is in the people of the States respectively; and the sovereign power of the United States would, for the same reason, be in "the people of the United States," if there were any such people, known as a single nation, and the framers of the federal government. We have already seen, however, that there are no such people, in a strict political sense, and that no such people had any agency in the formation of our Constitution, but that it was formed by *the States*, emphatically as such. It would be absurd, according to all principles received and acknowledged among us, to say that the sovereign power is in one party, and the power which creates the government is in another. The true sovereignty of the United States, therefore, is in the States, and not in the people of the United States, nor in the federal government. That government is but the agent through whom a portion of this sovereign power is exerted; possessing no sovereignty itself, and exerting no power, except such only as its constituents have conferred on it. In ascertaining what these powers are, it is obviously proper that we should look only to the grant from which they are derived. The agent can claim nothing for itself, and on its own account. The Constitution is a compact, and the parties to it are each State, with each and every other State. The federal government is not a party, but is the mere creature of the agreement between the States as parties. Each State is both grantor and grantee, receiving from each and all the other States precisely what, in its turn, it concedes to each and all of them. The rule, therefore, that the words are to be taken most strongly in favor of the grantee, cannot apply, because, as each State is both grantor and grantee, it would give exactly as much as it would take away. The only mode, therefore, by which we may be certain to do no injustice to the intentions of the parties, is by taking their *words* as the true exponents of their meaning.

Our author thinks, however, that a more liberal rule ought to be adopted, in construing the Constitution of the United States, because "the grant inures solely and exclusively for the benefit of the grantor himself"; and therefore he supposes that "no one would deny the propriety of giving to the words of the grant a benign and liberal interpretation." Admit that it is so, and it would seem to follow that "the benefit of the grantor" requires that we should take from him as little as possible, and that an "interpretation of the words of the grant" would not be "benign and liberal" as to him, if it deprived him of any more of his rights and powers, than his *own words* prove that he intended to relinquish. It is evident that this remark of the author proceeds upon the leading idea, that the people of the United States are the only party to the contract; an idea which, we have already seen, can by no means be justified or allowed. The States are parties; each agreeing with each, and all the rest, that it will exercise, through a common agent, precisely so much of its sovereign rights and powers, as will, in its own opinion, be beneficial to itself, when so exercised. The grant "inures to the sole and exclusive benefit of the grantor"; and who but the grantor himself shall determine what benefit he had in view, and how far the grant shall extend, in order to secure it? This he has done, in the case before us, by the very terms of the grant. If you hold him bound by anything beyond those terms, you enable others to decide this matter for him, and may thus virtually abrogate his contract, and substitute another in its place.

I certainly do not mean to say, that in construing the Constitution, we should at all times confine ourselves to its *strict letter*. This would, indeed, be *sticking in the bark*, to the worst possible purpose. Many powers are granted by that instrument, which are not included within its express terms, literally taken, but which are, nevertheless, within their obvious meaning. The strict construction for which I contend, applies to the *intention* of the framers of the Constitution; and this may or may not require a strict construction of their words.

There is no fair analogy as to this matter between the Federal Constitution and those of the States, although the author broadly asserts that they are not "distinguishable in this respect"; and this will sufficiently appear from the following considerations:

1. The entire sovereignty of each State is in the people thereof. When they form for themselves a constitution of government, they part with no portion of their sovereignty, but merely determine what portion thereof shall lie dormant, what portion they will exercise, and in what modes and by what agencies they will exercise it. There is but one party to such a government, to wit, the people of the

State. Whatever power their government may possess, it is still the power of the people; and their sovereignty remains the same. So far, therefore, there is "no solid objection to implied powers" in a *State* constitution; because, by employing power in the government, you take no power from those who made the government.

2. As government is the agent and representative of the sovereign power of the people, the *presumption* is, that they intend to make it the agent and representative of *all* their power. In every frame of limited government, the people deny to themselves the exercise of some portion of their rights and powers, but the *larger* portion never lies thus dormant. In this case, therefore, (viz.: of a government established by an aggregate people), the question naturally is, not what powers are *granted*, but what are *denied*; and the rule of strict construction, if applied at all, should be applied only to the powers denied. This would have the effect of enlarging the powers of government, by limiting the restraints imposed on it.

3. As it is fair to presume that a people absolutely sovereign, and having an unlimited right to govern themselves as they please, would not deny to themselves the exercise of any power necessary to their prosperity and happiness, we should admit all fair and reasonable implications in favor of the government, because, otherwise, some power necessary to the public weal, might be dormant and useless.

In these respects, there is no just analogy between the State constitutions and that of the United States.

In the first place, the Constitution of the United States is not a frame of government to which there is but one party. The States are parties, each stipulating and agreeing with each and all the rest. Their agreement is, that a certain portion of that power which each is authorized to exercise within its own limits shall be exercised by their common agent, within the limits of all of them. This is not the separate power of each, but the joint power of all. In proportion, therefore, as you increase the powers of the federal government, you necessarily detract from the separate powers of the States. We are not to *presume* that a sovereign people mean to surrender any of their powers; still less should we presume that they mean to surrender them, *to be exerted over themselves, by a different sovereignty*. In this respect, then, every reasonable implication is *against* the federal government.

In the second place, the Constitution of the United States is not the primary social relation of those who formed it. The State governments were already organized, and were adequate to all the purposes of their municipal concerns. The federal government was established only for such purposes as the State government could not answer, to wit, the common purposes of *all* the States. Whether, therefore, the powers of that government be greater or less, the *whole* power of the States, (or so much thereof as they design to exercise at all), is represented, either in the federal government or in their own. In this respect, therefore, there is no necessity to imply power in the federal government.

In the third place, whatever power the States have not delegated to the federal government, they have reserved to themselves. Every useful faculty of government is found either in the one or the other. Whatever the federal government cannot do for *all* the States, each State can do for itself, subject only to the restraints of its own constitution. No power, therefore, is dormant and useless, except so far only as the States voluntarily decline to exert it. In this respect, also, there is no necessity to imply power in the federal government.

In all these particulars the Federal Constitution is clearly "distinguishable from the constitutions of the State governments." The views just presented support this obvious distinction, that in the State constitutions every power is granted which is not denied; in the Federal Constitution, every power is denied which is not granted. There are yet other views of the subject, which lead us to the same conclusion.

The objects for which the federal government was established, are by no means equal in importance to those of the State constitutions.

A Brief Inquiry into the True Nature and Character of Our Federal Government
by Abel P. Upshur (1840)

It is difficult to imagine any necessity for a federal government at all, except what springs from the relations of the States to foreign nations. A union among them is undoubtedly valuable for many purposes. It renders them stronger and more able to resist their enemies; it attracts to them the respect of other countries, and gives them advantages in the formation of foreign connections; it facilitates all the operations of war, of commerce, and of foreign diplomacy. But these objects, although highly important, are not so important as those great rights which are secured to us by the State constitutions. The States might singly protect themselves; singly form their foreign connections, and singly regulate their commerce; not so effectually, it is true, but effectually enough to afford reasonable security to their independence and general prosperity. In addition to all this, we rely exclusively on the State governments for the security of the great rights of life, liberty and property. All the valuable and interesting relations of the social state spring from them. They give validity to the marriage tie; they prescribe the limits of parental authority; they enforce filial duty and obedience; they limit the power of the master, and exact the proper duties of the servant. Their power pervades all the ranks of society, restraining the strong, protecting the weak, succoring the poor, and lifting up the fallen and helpless. They secure to all persons an impartial administration of public justice. In all the daily business of life, we act under the protection and guidance of the State governments. They regulate and secure our rights of property; they enforce our contracts and preside over the peace and safety of our firesides. There is nothing dear to our feelings or valuable in our social condition, for which we are not indebted to their protecting and benignant action. Take away the federal government altogether, and still we are free, our rights are still protected, our business is still regulated, and we still enjoy all the other advantages and blessings of established and well-organized government. But if you take away the State governments, what have you left? A federal government, which can neither regulate your industry, secure your property, nor protect your person! Surely there can be no just reason for stealing, by liberal constructions and implications, from these beneficent State governments, any portion of their power, in order to confer it on another government, which, from its very organization, cannot possibly exert it for equally useful purposes. A strict construction of the Constitution will give to the federal government all the power which it can beneficially exert, all that it is necessary for it to possess, and all that its framers ever designed to confer on it.

To these views of the subject we may add, that there is a natural and necessary tendency in the federal government to encroach on the rights and powers of the States. As the representative of all the States, it affords, in its organization, an opportunity for those combinations by which a majority of the States may oppress the minority, against the spirit or even the letter of the Constitution. There is no danger that the federal government will ever be too weak. Its means of aggrandizing itself are so numerous, and its temptations to do so are so strong, that there is not the least necessity to *imply* any new power in its favor. The States, on the contrary, have no motive to encroach on the federal government, and no power to do so, even if they desired it. In order, therefore, to preserve the just balance between them, we should incline, in every doubtful case, in favor of the States; confident that the federal government has always the inclination, and always the means, to maintain itself in all its just powers.

The Constitution itself suggests that it should be strictly and not liberally construed. The tenth amendment provides, that "the powers not delegated to the United States, nor prohibited to the States, by the Constitution, are reserved to the States or the people." There was a corresponding provision in the articles of confederation, which doubtless suggested this amendment. It was considered necessary, in order to prevent that latitude of construction which was contended for by one of the great political parties of the country, and much dreaded and strenuously opposed by the other. In the articles of confederation all "rights, jurisdictions and powers" are reserved, except only such as are *expressly* delegated; but in the Constitution, the word "expressly" is omitted. Our author infers from this fact, that it was the intention of the framers of the tenth amendment to leave "the question, whether the particular power which is the subject of contest has been delegated to one government or prohibited to the other, to depend upon a fair construction of the whole instrument"; doubtless intending by the word "fair," a construction as *liberal* as would be applied to any other frame of government. This argument is much relied on, and is certainly not without plausibility, but it loses all its force, if the omission can be otherwise satisfactorily accounted for. The Constitution provides that congress shall have power to pass all laws which shall be necessary and proper for carrying into effect the various powers which it grants. If this clause confers no additional faculty of any sort, it is wholly useless and out of place; the fact that it is found in the Constitution is sufficient proof that some effect was intended to be given to it. It was contemplated that, in executing the powers expressly granted, it might be necessary to exert some power not *enumerated*, and as to which some doubt might, for that reason, be entertained. For example, the power to provide a navy is not, *in itself*, the power to build a dry dock; but, as dry docks are necessary and proper means for providing a navy, congress shall have power to authorize the construction of them. But if the word "expressly" had been used in the tenth amendment, it would have created a very rational and strong doubt of this. There would have been, at least, an *apparent* repugnance between the two provisions of the Constitution; not a *real* one, I admit, but still sufficiently probable to give rise to embarrassing doubts and disputes. Hence the necessity of omitting the word "expressly," in the tenth amendment. It left free from doubt and unaffected the power of congress to provide the necessary and proper means of executing the granted powers, while it denied to the federal government every power which was *not* granted. The same result was doubtless expected from this amendment of the Constitution, which was expected from the corresponding provision in the articles of confederation; and the difference in the terms employed is but the necessary consequence of the difference in other provisions of the two systems.

Strictly speaking, then, the Constitution allows no *implication* in favor of the federal government, in any case whatever. Every power which it can properly exert is a granted power. All these are *enumerated* in the Constitution, and nothing can be constitutionally done, beyond that enumeration, unless it be done as *a means* of executing some one of the enumerated powers. These means are *granted*, not implied; they are given as the necessary incidents of the power itself, or, more properly speaking, as component parts of it, because the power would be imperfect, nugatory and useless, without them. It is true, that in regard to these incidental powers, some discretion must, of necessity, be left with the government. But there is at the same time, a peculiar necessity that a strict construction should be applied to them; because that is the precise point at which the government is most apt to encroach. Without some strict, definite and fixed rules upon the subject, it would be left under no restraint, except what is imposed by its own wisdom, integrity and good faith. In proportion as a power is liable to be abused, should we increase and strengthen the checks upon it. And this brings us to the inquiry, what are these incidental powers, and by what rules are they to be ascertained and defined?

The only source from which these incidental powers are derived is that clause of the Constitution which confers on congress the power "to make all laws which are necessary and proper for carrying into execution the foregoing powers, and all other powers vested by this Constitution in the government of the United States, or in any department or officer thereof." The true character of this clause cannot be better given than in the words of the author himself: "It neither enlarges any power specifically granted, nor is it a grant of any new power to congress. But it is merely a declaration, for the removal of all uncertainty, that the means of carrying into execution, those otherwise granted, are included in the grant." His general reasoning upon the subject is very lucid, and, to a certain extent, correct and convincing. He contends that the word "necessary" is not to be taken in its restricted sense, as importing absolute and indispensable necessity, but is to be understood in the sense of "convenient," "useful," "requisite"; as being such that, without them, "the grant would be nugatory." The dangerous latitude implied by this construction, he thinks sufficiently restrained by the additional word "proper," which implies that the means shall be "constitutional and *bona fide* appropriate to the end." In all this he is undoubtedly correct; but the conclusion which he draws from it, cannot be so readily admitted. "If," says he, "there be any general principle which is inherent in the very definition of government, and essential to every step of the progress to be made by that of the United States, it is that every power vested in the government is, in its nature, sovereign, and includes, by force of the term, a right to employ all the means requisite, and fairly applicable to the attainment of the end of such power, unless they are excepted in the Constitution, or are immoral, or are contrary to the essential objects of political society." This is by no means a legitimate conclusion from his own fair and forcible reasoning. The doctrine here is, in effect, that the federal government is absolutely unrestricted in the selection and use of the means of executing its own powers, except only so far as those means are *excepted* in the Constitution. Whether or not they are "requisite," "fairly applicable to the attainment of the end of such power," "immoral or contrary to the essential objects of political society," all these are questions which the government alone can decide, and, of course, as their own judgment and discretion are their only rule, they are under no sort of limitation or control in these respects. The standards of political morality, of public convenience and necessity, and of conformity to the essential objects of society, are quite too fluctuating and indeterminate to be relied on, by a free people, as checks upon the power of their rulers. The only real restriction, then, which the author proposes in the above passage, is that which may be found in the fact, that the proposed means are "*excepted*" in the Constitution; and this is directly contrary to the letter and spirit of that instrument. The federal government possesses no power which is not "*delegated*"; "the powers not delegated to the United States by the Constitution, nor prohibited by it to the States, are reserved to the States respectively, or to the people." The author's idea is, that everything is granted which is not excepted; whereas, the language of the tenth amendment is express, that everything is excepted which is not granted. If the word "excepted" is to be understood in this sense, the author's idea is correct; but this does not accord with the general scope of his opinions and reasoning. He approaches much nearer to the true rule in the following passage. "Let the end be legitimate; let it be within the scope of the Constitution; and all means which are appropriate, which are plainly adapted to the end, and which are not prohibited, but *are consistent with the letter and spirit of the instrument*, are constitutional." The words in italics, are all important in the matter, and give to the passage a meaning wholly different from that of the passage first quoted.

The author's error is equally great, and far more dangerous, in supposing that the means of executing its powers are conferred on the *government*. The *general* proposition is true, as he has stated it; but it is not true in the application which he has made of it to *our* government. He regards the tenth amendment as altogether unnecessary, and tells us, in express terms, that the powers of the government would be exactly the same with or without it. This is a great and obvious mistake. The tenth amendment was wisely incorporated into the Constitution, for the express purpose of denying to the government that unbounded discretion, in the selection and use of its means, for which he contends. The power to make all laws necessary and proper for carrying into effect the granted powers is conferred on *congress* alone; it is exclusively a *legislative* power. So far, therefore, as the *government* is concerned, it derives no power from this clause; and the same is true of its several departments. They have no discretion in the selection of any incidental means of executing their several trusts. If they need the use of such means, they must apply to congress to furnish them; and it is discretionary with that body, whether to furnish them or not. All this is perfectly clear from the very language of the Constitution, and the propriety of such a provision must be apparent to everyone. If power could be implied in favor of such a government as ours, it would, if nothing were said to the contrary, be implied in favor of every department and officer thereof, to the execution of whose duties it might seem to be necessary. This would be a wide extent of discretion, indeed; so wide, that it would render all the limitations of the Constitution nugatory and useless. It is precisely this result which was intended to be prevented by the clause in question. The States were unwilling to entrust such a discretion either to the government, or to the several departments or officers thereof. They were willing to confer it on congress alone; on the legislative department, the more immediate representatives of the States and their people, who would be most apt to discharge the trust properly, because they had the least temptation to abuse it. It is not true, then, as our author supposes, or, at least, it is not true of *our* system, that "every power in the government is, in its nature, sovereign, and includes, by force of the term, a right to employ all the means requisite, and fairly applicable to the attainment of the ends of such power, unless they are excepted in the Constitution, or forbidden by some consideration of public morals, or by their unsuitableness to the proper objects of government." In our government, the means are at the disposal of one department only, which may either grant or withhold them at its pleasure.

What, then, are the proper limitations of the power of congress in this respect? This has always been a subject of great difficulty, and of marked difference of opinion, among politicians. I cannot hope that I shall be able perfectly to disembarrass it; but I think, nevertheless, that there are a few plain rules, the propriety of which all will admit, and which may materially aid us in the formation of a sound opinion upon the subject.

In the first place, then, it is to be observed that congress has no power under this clause of the Constitution, except to provide the *means* of executing the granted powers. It is not enough that the means adopted are sufficient to that end; they must be adopted *bona fide, with a view to accomplish it.* Congress have no right to use for the accomplishment of one purpose, means ostensibly provided for another. To do so would be a positive fraud, and a manifest usurpation; for, if the purpose be lawful, it may be accomplished by its own appropriate means, and if it be unlawful, it should not be accomplished at all. It is quite obvious that, without this check, congress may, by indirection, accomplish almost any forbidden object; for among the great variety of means adapted to carry out the granted powers, some may be found equally calculated to effect, either by their direct, or their indirect action, purposes of a wholly different character and tendency. It is, therefore, of the utmost importance to the preservation of the true principles of the Constitution, that strict faith should be kept upon this point.

In the second place, the means provided must not only be "necessary," but they must also be "proper." If the word "necessary" stood alone, it would be susceptible of a very extended meaning, and would probably be considered as embracing powers which it never was in the contemplation of the framers of the Constitution to grant. It was necessary, then, to limit and restrain it by some other word, and the word "proper" was very happily selected. This word requires that the means selected shall be strictly *constitutional*. In ascertaining this, we must have regard not only to the express provisions of the Constitution, but also to the general nature and character of our institutions. Ours is a *free* government, which implies that it is also an *equal* government; it therefore authorizes the employment of no means for the execution of its powers, except such as are consistent with the spirit of liberty and equality. Ours is a *confederated* government; it therefore authorizes no means which are inconsistent with the distinct sovereignty of the States, the confederating powers. Ours is a government of "delegated" powers, limited and specifically enumerated; it therefore authorizes no means which involve, in the use of them, any distinct substantive power, *not* granted. This single rule, if fairly and honestly observed, will go far to remove many serious difficulties upon this point, and will deprive the federal government of many important powers which it has hitherto exercised, and which are still claimed for it, by our author, and the whole political school to which he belongs. The propriety, and, indeed, the absolute necessity of the rule, appear to me to be obvious. If powers not granted might be used as means of executing the granted powers, it is manifest that no power whatever could be considered as denied. It is not enough that there is no apparent unconstitutionality in the use of such means, *in the particular case*. If they involve a principle which will authorize the use of ungranted powers in any *other* case, they are forbidden by the Constitution. To illustrate this idea by an example. Congress has power to regulate commerce among the several States. This is supposed by some to give them power to open channels of commerce, by making roads, cutting canals, &c., through the territories of the States. But this is a substantive power in itself, not granted to the United States, but reserved to the States respectively, and therefore is not allowed as a *means* of regulating commerce among the States. Let us suppose, however, that the opening of roads and cutting of canals are the *very best* means of facilitating and regulating commerce among the States, and that there is nothing in the *language* of the Constitution to forbid it; we are still to inquire what farther powers would be necessarily implied, as incidents of this. We find that the power to open a road through a State, implies the power to keep it in repair; to impose fines and penalties on those who injure it, and, consequently, to enforce those fines and penalties by the exercise of a jurisdiction over it. We find also, that the power to *make* such a road, implies the power to *locate* it; and, as there is nothing to control the discretion of congress in this respect, there is nothing to forbid them to locate *their* road, upon the bed of a State canal, or along the whole course of a State turnpike. The effect of this would be to transfer to the United States, against the consent of the State, and without compensation, improvements made by the State within her own territory and at her own expense. Nay, the supremacy claimed for the powers of congress in this respect would, upon the same principle, authorize them to run a road through the center of a State capitol, or to cover half her territory with roads and canals, over which the State could exert neither jurisdiction nor control. The improvements of individuals too, and of corporate bodies made under the authority of State laws, would thus be held at the mercy of the United States. When we see, then, that this means of regulating commerce among the States would necessarily imply these vast and forbidden powers, we should unhesitatingly reject them as unconstitutional. This single instance, given by way of example and illustration, presents a rule which, if strictly adhered to in all analogous cases, would go far to remove the difficulties, and to prevent the contests, which so often arise on this part of the Constitution.

These few simple rules are, in their nature, technical, and may at all times be easily applied, if congress will observe good faith in the exercise of its powers. There is another of a more enlarged and liberal character, which the word "proper" suggests, and which, if applied with sound judgment, perfect integrity and impartial justice, will render all others comparatively unnecessary. It exacts of congress an extended and fair view of the relations of all the States, and a strictly impartial regard to their respective rights and interests. Although the direct action of a granted power, by the *means also granted* in the Constitution, may be both unequal and unjust, those means would, nevertheless, be perfectly constitutional. Such injustice and inequality would be but the necessary consequence of that imperfection, which characterizes every human institution, and to which those who undertake to prescribe specific rules to themselves, are bound to submit. But when congress are called on to provide new means of executing a granted power, none are "proper," and therefore none are constitutional which operate unequally and unjustly, among the States or the people. It is true that perfect and exact equality in this respect is not to be expected; but a near approach to it will always be made, by a wise and fair legislation. Great and obvious injustice and inequality may at all times be avoided. No "means" which involve these consequences can possibly be considered "proper," either in a moral, or in a constitutional sense. It requires no high intellectual faculty to apply this rule; simple integrity is all that is required.

I have not thought it necessary to follow the author through his extended examination of what he terms the incidental powers of congress, arising under the clause of the Constitution we are examining. It would be indeed an endless task to do so; for I am unable to perceive that he proposes any limit to them at all. Indeed, he tells us in so many words, that "upon the whole, the result of the most careful examination of this clause is, that if it does not enlarge, it cannot be construed to restrain the powers of congress, or impair the right of the legislature to exercise its best judgment in the selection of measures to carry into execution the constitutional powers of the national government." This is, indeed, a sweep of authority, boundless and unrestricted. The "best judgment" of congress is the only limit proposed to its powers, whilst there is nothing to control that judgment, nor to correct its errors. Government is abandoned emphatically to its own discretion; for even if a corrective be supposed to exist with the people, that corrective can never be applied in behalf of an oppressed minority. Are the rules which I have proposed indeed nothing? Is no effect whatever to be given to this word "proper," in this clause of the Constitution? Can the author possibly be right in supposing that the Constitution would be the same without it as with it; and that the only object of inserting it was "the desire to remove all possible doubt respecting the right to legislate on that vast mass of incidental powers which must be involved in the Constitution, if that instrument be not a splendid pageant, or a delusive phantom of sovereignty"? It was, indeed, the object of the framers of the Constitution "to remove all possible doubt" from this subject. They desired neither a splendid pageant nor a splendid government. They knew that without this restriction ours would be both; and as powerful as splendid. They did not design that any power with which they thought proper to clothe it should be inoperative, for want of means to carry it into execution; but they never designed to give it the boundless field of its own mere will, for the selection of those means. Having specifically enumerated its powers, as far as was practicable, they never designed to involve themselves in the absurdity of removing, by a single clause, every restriction which they had previously imposed. They meant to assure their agent that, while none of the powers with which they had thought proper to clothe it should be nugatory, none of them should be executed by any means which were not both "necessary" and "proper."

The lovers of a strong consolidated government have labored strenuously, and I fear with too much success, to remove every available restriction upon the powers of congress. The tendency of their principles is to establish that legislative omnipotence which is the fundamental principle of the British Constitution, and which renders every form of *written* constitution idle and useless. They suffer themselves to be too much attracted by the splendors of a great central power. Dazzled by these splendors, they lose sight of the more useful, yet less ostentatious purposes of the State governments, and seem to be unconscious that, in building up this huge temple of federal power, they necessarily destroy those less pretending structures from which alone they derive shelter, protection and safety. This is the *ignis fatuus* which has so often deceived nations, and betrayed them into the slough of despotism. On all such, the impressive warning of Patrick Henry, drawn from the lessons of all experience, would be utterly lost. "Those nations who have gone in search of grandeur, power and splendor, have also fallen a sacrifice and been the victims of their own folly. While they acquired those visionary blessings, they lost their freedom." The consolidationists forget these wholesome truths, in their eagerness to invest the federal government with every power which is necessary to realize their visions in a great and splendid nation. Hence they do not discriminate between the several classes of federal powers, but contend for all of them, with the same blind and devoted zeal. It is remarkable that, in the exercise of all those functions of the federal government which concern our foreign relations, scarcely a case can be supposed, requiring the aid of any implied or incidental power, as to which any serious doubt can arise. The powers of that government, as to all such matters, are so distinctly and plainly pointed out in the very letter of the Constitution, and they are so ample for all the purposes contemplated, that it is only necessary to understand them according to their plain meaning, and to exercise them according to their acknowledged extent. No auxiliaries are required; the government has only to go on in the execution of its trusts, with powers at once ample and unquestioned. It is only in matters which concern our domestic policy, that any serious struggle for federal power has ever arisen, or is likely to arise. Here, that love of splendor and display, which deludes so large a portion of mankind, unites with that self-interest by which *all* mankind are swayed, in aggrandizing the federal government, and adding to its powers. He who thinks it better to belong to a splendid and showy government, than to a free and happy one, naturally seeks to surround all our institutions with a gaudy pageantry, which belongs only to aristocratic or monarchical systems. But the great struggle is for those various and extended powers, from the exercise of which *avarice* may expect its gratifications. Hence the desire for a profuse expenditure of public money, and hence the thousand schemes under the name of internal improvements, by means of which hungry contractors may plunder the public treasury, and wily speculators prey upon the less skillful and cunning. And hence, too, another sort of legislation, the most vicious of the whole, which, *professing* a fair and legitimate object of public good, looks, *really*, only to the promotion of private interests. It is thus that *classes* are united in supporting the powers of government, and an interest is created strong enough to carry all measures, and sustain all abuses.

Let it be borne in mind that, as to all these subjects of domestic concern, there is no absolute necessity that the federal government should possess any power at all. They are all such as the *State* governments are perfectly competent to manage; and the *most* competent, because each State is the best judge of what is useful or necessary to itself. There is, then, no room to complain of any want of power to do whatever the interests of the people require to be done. This is the topic upon which our author has lavishly expended his strength. Looking upon government as a machine contrived only for the public good, he thinks it strange that it should not be supposed to possess all the faculties calculated to answer the purposes of its creation. And surely it would be strange, if it were, indeed, so defectively constructed. But the author seems to forget that in our system the federal government stands not alone. That is but *a part* of the machine; complete in itself, certainly, and perfectly competent, without borrowing aid from any other source, to work out its own part of the general result. But it is not competent to work out the *whole* result. The State governments have also *their* part to perform, and the two together make the perfect work. Here, then, are all the powers which it is necessary that government should possess; not lodged in one place, but distributed; not the power of the State governments, nor of the federal government, but the aggregate of their several and respective powers. In the exercise of those functions which the State governments are forbidden to exercise, the federal government need not look beyond the letter of its charter for any needful power; and in the exercise of any other function, there is still less necessity that it should do so; because, whatever power that government does not plainly possess, is plainly possessed by the State governments. I speak, of course, of such powers only as may be exercised either by the one or the other, and not of such as are denied to both. I mean only to say, that so far as the States and the people have entrusted power to government at all, they have done so in language plain and full enough to render all implication unnecessary. Let the federal government exercise only such power as plainly belongs to it, rejecting all such as is even doubtful, and it will be found that our system will work out all the useful ends of government, harmoniously and without contest, and without dispute, and without usurpation.

{Chapter IX}

I have thus finished the examination of the *political* part of these commentaries, and this is the only object with which this review was commenced. There are, however, a few topics yet remaining, of great public concern, and which ought not to be omitted. Some of these, as it seems to me, have been presented by the author in false and deceptive lights, and others of them, from their intrinsic importance, cannot be too often pressed upon public attention. I do not propose to examine them minutely, but simply to present them in a few of their strongest lights.

In his examination of the structure and functions of the house of representatives, the author has given his views of that clause of the Constitution which allows representation to three-fifths of the slaves. He considers the compromise upon this subject as unjust in principle, and decidedly injurious to the people of the non-slaveholding States. He admits that an equivalent for this supposed concession to the South was intended to be secured by another provision, which directs that "Representatives and direct taxes shall be apportioned among the several States, according to their respective numbers"; but he considers this provision "more specious than solid; for while in the levy of taxes it apportions them on three-fifths of persons not free, it on the other hand, really exempts the other two-fifths from being taxed at all as property.

Whereas, if direct taxes had been apportioned, as upon principle they ought to be, according to the real value of property within the State, the whole of the slaves would have been taxable as property. But a far more striking inequality has been disclosed by the practical operations of the government. The principle of representation is constant and uniform; the levy of direct taxes is occasional and rare. In the course of forty years, no more than three direct taxes have been levied, and those only under very extraordinary and pressing circumstances. The ordinary expenditures of the government are, and always have been, derived from other sources.

Imposts upon foreign importations have supplied, and will generally supply, all the common wants; and if these should not furnish an adequate revenue, excises are next resorted to, as the surest and most convenient mode of taxation. Direct taxes constitute the last resort; and, as might have been foreseen, would never be laid until other resources had failed."

This is a very imperfect, and, as it seems to me, not a very candid view of a grave and important subject. It would have been well to avoid it altogether, if it had been permitted; for the public mind needs no encouragement to dwell, with unpleasant reflections, upon the topics it suggests. In an examination of the Constitution of the United States, however, some notice of this peculiar feature of it was unavoidable; but we should not have expected the author to dismiss it with such criticism only as tends to show that it is unjust to his own peculiar part of the country. It is manifest to everyone that the arrangement rests upon no particular principle, but is a mere compromise between conflicting interests and opinions. It is much to be regretted that it is not on all hands acquiesced in and approved, upon that ground; for no public necessity requires that it should be discussed, and it cannot now be changed without serious danger to the whole fabric. The people of the slave-holding States themselves have never shown a disposition to agitate the question at all, but, on the contrary, have generally sought to avoid it. It has, however, always "been complained of as a grievance," by the non-slaveholding States, and that too in language which leaves little doubt that a wish is very generally entertained to change it. A grave author, like Judge Story, who tells the people, as it were *ex cathedra*, that the thing is unjust in itself, will scarcely repress the dissatisfaction, which such an announcement, falling in with preconceived opinions, will create, by a simple recommendation to acquiesce in it as a compromise, tending upon the whole to good results. His remarks may render the public mind more unquiet than it now is; they can scarcely tranquillize or reconcile it. For myself, I am very far from wishing to bring the subject into serious discussion, with any view to change; but I cannot agree that an arrangement, obviously *injurious* to the South, should be held up as giving her advantages of which the North has reason to complain.

I will not pause to inquire whether the rule apportioning representatives according to *numbers*, which, after much contest, was finally adopted by the convention, be the correct one or not. Supposing that it is so, the rule which apportions *taxation* in the same way, follows as matter of course. The difficulties under which the convention seem to have labored, in regard to this subject, may well excite our surprise, at the present day. If the North really supposed that they conceded anything to the South, by allowing representation to three-fifths of their slaves, they were certainly but poorly compensated for the concession, by that provision of the Constitution which apportions taxation according to representation. This principle was universally acknowledged throughout the United States, and is, in fact, only a modification of the great principle upon which the revolution itself was based. That taxation should be apportioned to representation, results from the federative character of our government; and the fact that this rule was adopted, sustains the views which have been presented, upon this point. It would have been indeed strange, if some one State, having only half the representatives of its neighbor State, might yet have been subjected to twice the amount of taxation; Delaware, for instance, with her one representative, to twice the taxes of Pennsylvania, with her twenty-eight. A different rule from that which prevails might subject the weaker States to intolerable oppression. A combination among a few of the strongest States might, by a little management, throw the whole burden of taxation upon the others, by selecting only such subjects of taxation as they themselves did not possess, or which they possessed only to a comparatively small extent. It never would have answered to entrust the power of taxation to congress, without some check against these and similar abuses, and no check could have been devised, more effective or more appropriate than the provision now under consideration. All the States were interested in it; and the South much more deeply than the North. The slaves of the South afford the readiest of all possible subjects for this sort of practice; and it would be going too far to say that they would not, at some day or other, be selected for it, if this provision of the Constitution did not stand in the way. The Southern States would certainly never have adopted the Constitution, without some such guaranty as this, against those oppressions to which their peculiar institutions exposed them; and the weaker States, whether north or south, would never have adopted it, because it might lead to their utter annihilation in the confederacy. This provision of the Constitution, therefore, can scarcely be considered as an *equivalent* for anything conceded by some of the States to others. It resulted necessarily from the very nature of their union: it is an appropriate and necessary feature in every confederacy between sovereign States. We ought, then, to regard that provision of the Constitution, which allows representation to only three-fifths of the slaves, as a *concession made by the South*; and one for which they received no equivalent, except in the harmony which it served to produce.

Reverting to the rule, that representation shall be apportioned to population, and supposing that all parties acquiesce in the propriety of it, upon what principle is the rule itself founded? We have already seen that the whole country had adopted the principle, that *taxation* should be apportioned to representation, and, of course, in fixing the principle of representation, the question of taxation was necessarily involved. There is no perfectly just rule of taxation, but *property*; every man should contribute to the support of the government, according to his ability, that is, according to the value of that property to which government extends its protection. But this rule never can be applied in practice; because it is impossible to discover what is the amount of the property, either of individuals or nations. In regard to states, *population* is the best measure of this value which can be found, and is, in most cases, a sufficiently accurate one. Although the wealth of a state cannot be ascertained, its people can be easily counted, and hence the number of its people gives the best rule for its representation, and consequently, for its taxation.

The population of a state is received as the best measure of the value of its property, because it is in general true, that the greater the number of people, the greater is the amount of productive industry. But of what consequence is it, by *what sort of people* this amount of production is afforded? It was required that each State of our Union should contribute its due proportion to the common treasury; a proportion ascertained by the number of its people. Of what consequence is it, whether this contribution be made by the labor of slaves, or by that of freemen? All that the States had a right to require of one another was, that each should contribute its allotted proportion; but no State had a right to inquire from what particular sources that contribution arose. Each State having a perfect right to frame its own municipal regulations for itself, the other States had no right to subject her to any disabilities or disadvantages on account of them. If Massachusetts had a right to object to the representation of the slaves of Virginia, Virginia had the same right to object to the representation of the apprentices, the domestic servants, or even the mechanics of Massachusetts. The peculiar private condition and relations of the people of a State to one another could not properly be inquired into by any other State. That is a subject which each State regulates for itself; and it cannot enter into the question of the influence which such State ought to possess, in the common government of all the States. It is enough that the State brings into the common stock a certain amount of wealth, resulting from the industry of her people. Whether those people be men or women, bond or free, or bound to service for a limited time only, is the exclusive concern of the State itself, and is a matter with which the other States cannot intermeddle, without impertinence, injustice and oppression. So far, then, from limiting representation to three-fifths of the slaves, they ought *all* to be represented, for all contribute to the aggregate of the productive industry of the country. And, even then, the rule would operate injuriously upon the slave-holding States; for, if the labor of a slave be as productive as that of a free man, (and in agriculture it is so,) the cost of supporting him is much less. Therefore, of the same amount of food and clothing, raised by the two classes, a greater surplus will remain of that of the slave, and of course a greater amount subject to the demands of the public necessities.

The remarks of John Adams, delivered in convention,* are very forcible upon this point. According to Mr. Jefferson's report of them, he observed, "that the numbers of people are taken as an index of the wealth of the state, and not as subjects of taxation; that, as to this matter it was of no consequence by what name you called your people, whether by that of freemen or of slaves; that in some countries the laboring poor are called freemen, in others they are called slaves; but that the difference, as to the state, was imaginary only. What matters it whether a landlord, employing ten laborers on his farm, gives them annually as much money as will buy them the necessaries of life, or gives them those necessaries at short hand? The ten laborers add as much wealth to the state, increase its exports as much, in the one case as in the other. Certainly five hundred freemen produce no more profits, no greater surplus for the payment of taxes, than five hundred slaves. Therefore the State, in which are the laborers called freemen, should be taxed no more than that in which are the laborers called slaves. Suppose by an extraordinary operation of nature or of law, one-half the laborers of a State could, in the course of one night, be transformed into slaves, would the State be made poorer or less able to pay taxes? That the condition of the laboring poor in most countries, that of the fishermen particularly of the Northern States, is as abject as that of slaves. It is the number of laborers which produces the surplus for taxation, and numbers therefore, indiscriminately, are the fair index to wealth."

It is obvious that these remarks were made for a very different purpose from that which I have in view. The subject then before the convention was the proper rule of taxation, and it was Mr. Adams' purpose to show that, as to *that* matter, slaves should be considered only as *people*, and, consequently, as an index of the amount of taxable wealth. The convention had not *then* determined that representatives and direct taxes should be regulated by the same ratio. When they did determine this, the remarks of Mr. Adams seem to me conclusive, to show that representation of *all* the slaves ought

---

* Mr. Adams was not a member of the convention. This speech was made in congress in deliberating on the articles of confederation.

to have been allowed; nor do I see how those who held his opinions could possibly have voted otherwise. If slaves are *people*, as forming the measure of national wealth, and consequently of taxation, and if taxation and representation be placed upon the same principle, and regulated by the same ratio, then that slaves are people, in fixing the ratio of representation, is a logical *sequitur* which no one can possibly deny.

But it is objected that slaves are *property*, and, for that reason, are not more entitled to representation than any other species of property. But they are also *people*, and, upon analogous principles, are entitled to representation as people. It is in this character alone that the non-slave-holding States have a right to consider them, as has already been shown, and in this character alone is it *just* to consider them. "We ought to presume that every slave occupies a place which, but for his presence, would be occupied by a free white man; and, if this were so, every one, and not three-fifths only, would be represented. But the States who hold no slaves have no right to complain that this is not the case in other States, so long as the labor of the slave contributes as much to the common stock of productive industry, as the labor of the white man. It is enough that a State possesses a certain number of *people*, of living, rational beings. We are not to inquire whether they be black, or white, or tawny, nor what are their peculiar relations among one another. If the slave of the south be property, of what nature is that property, and what kind of interest has the owner in it? He has a right to the profits of the slave's labor. And so, the master of an indented apprentice has a right to the profits of *his* labor. It is true, one holds the right for the life of the slave, and the other only for a time limited in the apprentices' indentures; but this is a difference only in the *extent*, and not in the *nature* of the interest. It is also true, that the owner of a slave has, in most States, a right to *sell* him; but this is only because the laws of the State authorize him to do so. And, in like manner, the indentures of an apprentice may be transferred if the laws of the State will allow it. In all these respects, therefore, the slave and the indented apprentice stand upon precisely the same principle. To a certain extent, they are both property, and neither of them can be regarded as a free man; and if the one be not entitled to representation, the other also should be denied that right. Whatever be the difference of their relations to the separate members of the community, in the eye of that community they are both *people*. Here, again, Mr. Adams shall speak for me; and our country has produced few men who could speak more wisely. "A slave may indeed, from the custom of speech, be more properly called the wealth of his master, than the free laborer might be called the wealth of his employer; but as to the State, both are equally its wealth, and should therefore equally add to the quota of its tax." Yes; and, consequently, they should equally add to the quota of its *representation*.

Our author supposes that it is a great advantage to the slave-holding States that, while three-fifths of the slaves are entitled to representation, *two*-fifths are exempted from taxation. Why confine it to three-fifths? Suppose that *none* of them were entitled to representation, the only consequence would be, that the State would have fewer representatives, and, for that reason, would have a less amount of taxes to pay. In this case, *all* the slaves would be exempted from taxation; and, according to our author, the slave-holding States would have great reason to be content with so distinguishing an advantage. And, for the same reason, every other State would have cause to rejoice at the diminution of the number of its people, for although its *representation* would thereby be decreased, its *taxes* would be decreased in the same proportion. This is the true mode of testing the author's position. It will be found that every State values the right of representation at a price infinitely beyond the amount of direct taxes to which that right may subject it; and, of course, the Southern States have little reason to be thankful that two-fifths of their slaves are exempted from taxation, since they lose, in consequence of it, the right of representation to the same extent. The author, however, seems to have forgotten this connection between representation and taxation; he looks only at the sources whence the Union may draw wealth from the South, without inquiring into the principles upon which her representation may be enlarged.

A Brief Inquiry into the True Nature and Character of Our Federal Government
by Abel P. Upshur (1840)

He thinks that direct taxes ought to be apportioned, "according to the real value of property within the State"; in which case "the whole of the slaves would have been taxable as property." I have already remarked that this is, indeed, the true rule; but it is wholly impracticable. It would be alike impossible to fix a satisfactory standard of valuation, and to discover the taxable subjects. No approximation to the truth could be hoped for, without a host of officers, whose compensations would consume a large proportion of the tax, while, from the very nature of their duties, they would be forced into minute examinations, inconsistent with the freedom of our institutions, harassing and vexatious in their details, and leading inevitably to popular resistance and tumult. And this process must be gone through at every new tax; for the relative wealth of the States would be continually changing. Hence, *population* has been selected as the proper measure of the wealth of the States. But, upon our author's principle, the South would be, indeed, little better off than the lamb in the embrace of the wolf. The slaves are easily found; they can neither be buried under ground, nor hid in the secret drawers of a bureau. They are *peculiar*, too, to a particular region; and other regions, having none of them, would yet have a voice in fixing their value as subjects of taxation. That they would bear something more than their due share of this burden, is just as certain as that man, under all circumstances, will act according to his nature. In the meantime, not being considered as *people*, they would have no right to be heard in their own defense, through their representatives in the federal councils. On the other hand, the non-slave-holding States would be represented in proportion to the whole numbers of their people, and would be taxed only according to that part of their wealth which they might choose to disclose, or which they could not conceal. And in the estimate of this wealth, their *people* would not be counted as taxable subjects, although they hold to their respective States precisely the same relation, as laborers and contributors to the common treasury, as is held by the slaves of the South to their respective States. The rule, then, which considers slaves only as property to be taxed, and not as people to be represented, is little else than a rule imposing on the Southern States almost the entire burdens of the government, and allowing to them only the shadow of influence in the measures of that government.

The truth is, the slave-holding States have always contributed more than their just proportion to the wealth and strength of the country, and not *less* than their just proportion to its intelligence and public virtue. This is the only perfectly just measure of political influence; but it is a measure which cannot be applied in practice. We receive *population* as the best practicable substitute for it; and as all *people*, whatever be their private and peculiar conditions and relations, are presumed to contribute their share to the stock of general wealth, intelligence and virtue, they are all entitled to their respective shares of influence in the measures of government. The slave-holding States, therefore, had a right to demand that *all* their slaves should be represented; they yielded too much in agreeing that only three-fifths of them should possess that right. I cannot doubt that this would have been conceded by the convention, had the principle, that representatives and direct taxes should be apportioned according to the same ratio, been then adopted into the Constitution. It would have been perceived that, while the representation of the Southern States would thus have been increased, their share of the public taxes would have been increased in the same proportion; and thus they would have stood, in all respects, upon the same footing with the other States.

The Northern States would have said to them, "Count your people; it is of no consequence to us what is their condition at home; they are *laborers*, and therefore they contribute the same amount of taxable subjects, whether black or white, bond or free. We therefore recognize them as *people*, and give them representation as such. All that we require is, that when we come to lay direct taxes, they shall be regarded as people still, and you shall contribute for them precisely as we contribute for our people." This is the plain justice of the case; and this alone would be consistent with the great principles which ought to regulate the subject. It is a result which is no longer attainable, and the South will, as they ought to do, acquiesce in the arrangement as it now stands. But they have reason to complain that grave authors, in elaborate works designed to form the opinions of rising generations, should so treat the subject as to create an impression that the Southern States are enjoying advantages under our Constitution, to which they are not fairly entitled, and which they owe only to the liberality of the other States; for the South feels that these supposed advantages are, in fact, *sacrifices*, which she has made only to a spirit of conciliation and harmony, and which neither justice nor sound principle would ever have exacted of her.

The most defective part of the Federal Constitution, beyond all question, is that which relates to the executive department. It is impossible to read that instrument, without being forcibly struck with the loose and unguarded terms in which the powers and duties of the President are pointed out. So far as the legislature is concerned, the limitations of the Constitution are, perhaps, as precise and strict as they could safely have been made; but in regard to the executive, the convention appear to have studiously selected such loose and general expressions, as would enable the President, by implication and construction, either to neglect his duties, or to enlarge his powers. We have heard it gravely asserted in congress, that whatever power is neither legislative nor judiciary, is, of course, executive, and, as such, belongs to the President, under the Constitution! How far a majority of that body would have sustained a doctrine so monstrous, and so utterly at war with the whole genius of our government, it is impossible to say; but this, at least, we know, that it met with no rebuke from those who supported the particular act of executive power, in defense of which it was urged. Be this as it may, it is a reproach to the Constitution, that the executive trust is so ill-defined, as to leave any plausible pretense, even to the insane zeal of party devotion, for attributing to the President of the United States the powers of a despot; powers which are wholly unknown in any limited monarchy in the world.

It is remarkable that the Constitution is wholly silent in regard to the power of removal from office. The *appointing* power is in the President and senate; the President nominating, and the senate confirming; but the power to *remove* from office seems never to have been contemplated by the convention at all, for they have given no directions whatever upon the subject. The consequence has been precisely such as might have been expected, a severe contest for the possession of that power, and the ultimate usurpation of it, by that department of the government to which it ought never to be entrusted. In the absence of all precise directions upon the subject, it would seem that the power to remove ought to attend the power to appoint; for those whose duty it is to fill the offices of the country with competent incumbents, cannot possibly execute that trust fully and well, unless they have power to correct their own errors and mistakes, by removing the unworthy, and substituting better men in their places. This, I have no doubt, is the true construction of our Constitution. It was for a long time strenuously contended for by a large party in the country, and was finally yielded, rather to the confidence which the country reposed in the virtues of Washington, than to any conviction that it was properly an executive power, belonging only to the President. It is true of Washington alone of all the truly great of the earth, that he never inflicted an injury upon his country, except only such as proceeded from the excess of his own virtues. His known patriotism, wisdom and purity, inspired us with a confidence and a feeling of security against the abuses of power, which has led to the establishment of many precedents, dangerous to public liberty in the hands of any other man. Of these, the instance before us is not the least important. The power to remove from office is, in effect, the power to appoint to office. What does it avail that the senate must be consulted in appointing to office, if the President may, the very next moment, annul the act by removing the person appointed! The senate has no right to select; they can do nothing more than confirm or reject the person nominated by the President. The President may nominate his own devoted creatures; if the senate should disapprove any one of them, he has only to nominate another, and another, and another; for there is no danger that the list will be exhausted, until the senate will be persuaded or worried into compliance. And when the appointment is made, the incumbent knows that he is a mere tenant at will, and necessarily becomes the mere tool and slave of the man at whose sole pleasure

A Brief Inquiry into the True Nature and Character of Our Federal Government
by Abel P. Upshur (1840)

he eats his daily bread. Surely, it is a great and alarming defect in our Constitution, that so vast and dangerous a power as this should be held by one man. Nothing more is required to place the liberties of the country at the feet of the President, than to authorize him to fill, and to vacate and to fill again, at his sole will and pleasure, all the offices of the country.

The necessary consequence of enabling the President to remove from office at his mere pleasure is, that the officer soon learns to consider himself the officer of the President, and not of the country. The nature of his responsibility is changed; he answers not to the people for his conduct, for he is beyond their reach; he looks only to the President, and, satisfied with *his* approval, is regardless of everything else. In fact, his office, however obscure it may be, soon comes to be considered only a part of the great executive power lodged in the President. The President is the village postmaster, the collector of the customs, the marshal, and everything else; and the incumbents of those offices are but *his* agents, through whom, for the sake of convenience, he exercises so much of his gigantic powers. One step farther, and the agency of the senate in these appointments will be no longer invoked. A little more of that construction and implication to which the looseness of the Constitution, on this point, holds out the strongest invitation, and the President will say to the senate, "This collectorship is a part of the great executive trust which is lodged in me; I have a right to discharge it in person, if I please, and, consequently, I have a right to discharge it by my own agent. It is my duty to see that the laws are executed; and if I do so, that is all that the country can require of me. I have a right to do so in my own way." There is no extravagance in this supposition; nothing in the past history of the country which teaches us to consider it an improbable result. Who does not perceive that the claims which have already been made, in behalf of executive power upon this very point, must of necessity change the whole nature and spirit of our institutions? Their fundamental principle is, that all power is in *the people*, and that public officers are but their trustees and servants, responsible to *them* for the execution of their trusts. And yet, in the various ramifications of the executive power, in the thousand agencies necessary to the convenience and interests of the people, which belong to that department, there is, in effect, no responsibility whatever. The injured citizen can make his complaint only to the President, and the President's creature knows that he is perfectly secure of his protection, because he has already purchased it by slavish subserviency. Is it enough that the President himself is responsible? We shall soon see that his responsibility is nominal only; a mere formal mockery. And responsible for what? Will you impeach the President because a postmaster has robbed the public mail, or a collector of the customs stolen the public money? There is absurdity in the very idea. Will you impeach him because he does not remove these unfaithful agents, and appoint others? He will tell you that, according to the construction which has been given to the Constitution, and in which you yourselves have acquiesced, that matter depends solely on his own will, and you have no right to punish him for what the Constitution authorizes him to do. What then is the result? The President claims every power which, by the most labored constructions, and the most forced implications, can be considered as executive. No matter in how many hands they are distributed, he wields them all; and when we call on him to answer for an abuse of those powers, he gravely tells us, that his agents have abused them, and not he. And when we call on those agents to answer, they impudently reply, that it is no concern of ours, they will answer to the President! Thus powers may be multiplied and abused without end, and the people, the real sovereigns, the depositaries of all power, can neither check nor punish them!

This subject certainly calls loudly for public attention. We ought not to lose sight of the rapid progress we have made in the decline of public virtue. It becomes us to understand that we have, no longer, Washingtons among us, to whose pure hands the greatest powers may be safely entrusted. We are now in that precise stage of our progress, when reform is not impossible, and when the practical operation of the government has shown us in what particulars reform is necessary. If we regard our government, not as the mere institution of the hour, but as a system which is to last through many successive generations, protecting and blessing them, it becomes us to correct its faults, to prune its redundancies, to supply its defects, to strengthen its weak points, and check its tendency to run into irresponsible power. If this be not speedily done, it requires no prophet's eye to see that it will not be done at all. And whenever this great and necessary work shall be undertaken, the single reform which is here suggested will accomplish half that is required.

Another striking imperfection of the Constitution, as respects the executive department, is found in the veto power. The right to forbid the people to pass whatever laws they please, is the right to deprive them of self-government. It is a power which can never be entrusted to one man, or any number of men short of the people themselves, without the certain destruction of public liberty. It is true that each department of the government should be armed with a certain power of self-protection against the assaults of the other departments; and the executive, probably, stands most in need of such protection. But the veto power, as it stands in the Constitution, goes far beyond this object. It is, in effect, a power in the executive department to forbid all action in any other. It is true that, notwithstanding the veto of the President, a law may still be passed, provided *two-thirds* of each house of congress agree therein; but it is obvious that the cases are very rare, in which such concurrence could be expected. In cases of plain necessity or policy the veto would not be applied; and those of doubtful necessity or policy would rarely be carried by a majority so large as two-thirds of each house. And yet in these it may be just as important that the public will should be carried out, as in cases of less doubt and difficulty. It may be, also, that a President may oppose the passage of laws of the plainest and most pressing necessity. And if he should do so, it would certainly give him a most improper power over the people, to enable him to prevent the most necessary legislation, with only one-third of each house of congress in his favor. There is something incongruous in this union of legislative and executive powers in the same man. Perhaps it is proper that there should be a power somewhere, to check hasty and ill-considered legislation, and that power may be as well entrusted to the President as to any other authority. But it is not necessary that it should be great enough to prevent *all* legislation, nor to control in any respect the free exercise of the legislative will. It would be quite enough for the security of the rights of the executive, and quite enough to ensure temperate and wise legislation, to authorize the President merely to send back to the legislature for reconsideration any law which he disapproved. By thus affording to that body time and opportunity for reflection, with all the additional lights which the President himself could throw upon the subject, we should have every reasonable security for the due exercise of the legislative wisdom, and a fair expression of the public will. But if, after all this, the legislature, in both its branches, should still adhere to their opinion, the theory and the sound practice of all our institutions require that their decision should be binding and final.

But the great defect of the Constitution in relation to this department is, that the responsibility of the President is not duly secured. I am sensible of the great difficulty which exists in arranging this subject properly. It is scarcely possible to lodge the power of impeachment anywhere, without subjecting it to the danger of corrupting influences; and it is equally difficult so to limit the extent and direct the exercise of that power, as to reconcile a proper responsibility in the officer, with a proper independence and sense of security, in the discharge of his duties. The power to try impeachments is correctly lodged with the senate, the representative of the States; for, as the government, with all its offices, was created by the States, the States alone should have the right to try and to remove the delinquent incumbents. But in the exercise of this power, the concurrence of too large a proportion is made necessary to conviction. The same reasoning applies here which was applied to the veto power. Nothing short of the most flagrant and indisputable guilt will ever subject a president to removal by impeachment. He must be, indeed, but little practiced in the ways of men, or strangely misled and infatuated, if, with all the means which his office places within his control, he cannot bring over at least one-third of the senate to his support.

A Brief Inquiry into the True Nature and Character of Our Federal Government
by Abel P. Upshur (1840)

It is scarcely to be supposed that a man elected by the suffrages of a majority of the States would, within the short period of four years, so far forfeit his standing with the public, as not to retain the confidence of at least one-third of them. Besides, he has abundant means of influencing the *conduct* of his triers, however strong may be public opinion against him. To require, therefore, the concurrence of two-thirds of the senators present, is, in effect, to render the whole process an idle form. It might not be safe, however, to repose this high trust in a bare majority. The object to be attained is, on the one hand, to make the number authorized to convict so large, as to afford a reasonable assurance that there will be no conviction without clear proof of guilt, and, on the other, to make it so small, as to afford equal assurance that the guilty will not escape. I do not pretend to suggest how large the majority ought to be, in order to ensure this result; but it is perfectly certain that, as the matter now stands, in nine-tenths of the cases in which the power may be called into exercise, it will be found utterly unavailing for any good purpose. Indeed, it can scarcely fail to be extremely mischievous; for a charge of guilt preferred, and not sustained, will always strengthen the President, by enlisting public sympathy in his favor, and will thus indirectly sanction the very abuse for which he was subjected to trial. A President tried and acquitted will always be more powerful than he would have been, had he done nothing to bring his conduct into question.

There is a species of responsibility to which the President is subjected, in the fact that the people may refuse to re-elect him. This will certainly be felt in some degree, by those Presidents for whom a re-election possesses greater charms than any possible abuse of power. But this is, under any circumstances, a feeble security to the people; and it will be found of no value whatever, as soon as the government shall have approached a little nearer, than at present, to the confines of absolute power. Besides, the reasoning could not apply to a President in his second term, and who, according to the established usage, could not expect to be re-elected. This is the period through which he may revel in all the excesses of usurped authority, without responsibility, and almost without check or control.

The re-eligibility of the President, from term to term, is the necessary source of numberless abuses. The fact that the same President may be elected, not for a second term only, but for a third, or fourth, or twentieth, will ere long suggest to him the most corrupting uses of his powers, in order to secure that object. At present there is no danger of this. Presidents are now made, not by the free suffrages of the people, but by party management; and there are always more than one in the successful party, who are looking to their own turn in the presidential office. It is too early yet for a monopoly of that high honor; but the time will come, when the actual incumbent will find means to buy off opposition, and to ensure a continuance in office, by prostituting the trusts which belong to it. This is so obviously within the natural course of things, that it may well excite our surprise that the convention should have left the public liberty wholly unguarded, at so assailable a point. It is surely a plain dictate of wisdom, and a necessary provision in every free government, that there should be some definite limit to the duration of executive power, in the same hands. We cannot hope to be free from the corruptions which result from an abuse of presidential power and patronage, until that officer shall be eligible only for *one* term – a long term if you please – and until he shall be rendered more easily and directly responsible to the power which appoints him.

Regarding this work of Judge Story as a whole, it is impossible not to be struck with the laborious industry which he has displayed, in the collection and preparation of his materials. He does not often indulge himself in speculations upon the *general* principles of government, but confines himself, with great strictness, to the particular form before him. Considering him as a mere lawyer, his work does honor to his learning and research, and will form a very useful addition to our law libraries. But it is not in this light only that we are to view it. The author is a *politician*, as well as a lawyer, and has taken unusual pains to justify and recommend his own peculiar opinions. This he has done, often at the expense of candor and fairness, and, almost invariably, at the expense of historical truth. We may well doubt, therefore, whether his book will not produce more evil than good, to the country; since the false views which it presents, of the nature and character of our government, are calculated to exert an influence over the public mind, too seriously mischievous to be compensated by any new lights which it sheds upon other parts of our Constitution. Indeed, it is little else than a labored panegyric upon that instrument. Having made it, by forced constructions, and strange misapprehensions of history, to conform to his own *beau ideal* of a perfect government, he can discern in it nothing that is deficient, nothing that is superfluous. And it is his particular pleasure to arm it with strong powers, and surround it with imposing splendors. In his examination of the legislative department, he has displayed an extraordinary liberality of concession, in this respect. There is not a single important power ever exercised or claimed for congress, which he does not vindicate and maintain. The long-contested powers to protect manufactures, to construct roads, with an endless list of similar objects to which the public money may be applied, present no serious difficulty to his mind. An examination of these several subjects, in detail, would swell this review beyond its proper limits, and is rendered unnecessary by the great principles which it has been my object to establish. I allude to them here, only as illustrating the general character of this book, and as showing the dangerous tendency of its political principles. It is, indeed, a strong argument in favor of federal power; and when we have said this, we have given it the character which the author will most proudly recognize. And it is not for the legislature alone, that these unbounded powers are claimed; the other departments come in for a full share of his favor. Even when he is forced to condemn, he does it with a censure so faint, and so softened and palliated, as to amount to positive praise.

It is too late for the people of these States to indulge themselves in these undiscriminating eulogies of their Constitution. We have, indeed, every reason to admire and to love it, and to place it far above every other system, in all the essentials of good government. Still, it is far from being perfect, and we should be careful not to suffer our admiration of what is undoubtedly good in it, to make us blind to what is as undoubtedly evil. When we consider the difficulties under which the convention labored, the great variety of interests and opinions which it was necessary for them to reconcile, it is matter of surprise that they should have framed a government so little liable to objection. But the government which they framed is not that which our author has portrayed. Even upon the guarded principles for which I have contended in this review, the action of the whole system tends too strongly towards consolidation. Much of this tendency, it is true, might be corrected by ordinary legislation; but, even then, there would remain in the federal government an aggregate of powers, which nothing but an enlightened and ever-vigilant public opinion could confine within safe limits. But if our author's principles be correct, if ours be, indeed, a consolidated and not a federative system, I, at least, have no praises to bestow on it. Monarchy in form, open and acknowledged, is infinitely preferable to monarchy in disguise.

The principle that ours is a consolidated government of all the people of the United States, and not a confederation of sovereign States, must necessarily render it little less than omnipotent. That principle, carried out to its legitimate results, will assuredly render the federal government the strongest in the world. The powers of such a government are supposed to reside in *a majority of the people*; and, as its responsibility is only to the people, that majority may make it whatever they please. To whom is that majority itself responsible? Upon the theory that it possesses all the powers of the government, there is nothing to check, nothing to control it. In a population strictly homogeneous in interests, character and pursuits, there is no danger in this principle. We adopt it in all our State governments, and in them it is the true principle; because the majority can pass no law which will not affect themselves, in mode and degree, precisely as it affects others. But in a country so extensive as the United States, with great differences of character, interests and pursuits, and with these differences, too, marked by geographical lines, a fair opportunity is afforded for the exercise of an oppressive tyranny, by the majority over the minority. Large masses of mankind are not apt to be swayed, except by interest alone; and wherever that interest is distinct and clear, it presents a motive of action too strong to be controlled. Let it be supposed that a certain number of States, containing a majority of the people of all the States, should find it to their interest to pass laws oppressive to the minority, and violating their rights as secured by the Constitution. What redress is there, upon the principles of our author? Is it to be found in the federal tribunals? They are themselves a part of the oppressing government, and are, therefore, not impartial judges of the powers of that government. Is it to be found in the virtue and intelligence of the people? This is the author's great reliance. He acknowledges that the system, as he understands it, is liable to great abuses; but he supposes that the virtue and intelligence of the people will, under all circumstances, prove a sufficient corrective. Of what people? Of that very majority who have committed the injustice complained of, and who, according to the author's theory, are the sole judges whether they have power to do it or not, and whether it be injustice or not. Under such a system as this, it is a cruel mockery to talk of the rights of the minority. If they possess rights, they have no means to vindicate them. The majority alone possess the government; they alone measure its powers, and wield them without control or responsibility. This is despotism of the worst sort, in a system like ours. More tolerable, by far, is the despotism of one man, than that of a party, ruling without control, consulting its own interests, and justifying its excesses under the name of republican liberty. Free government, so far as its protecting power is concerned, is made for minorities alone.

But the system of our author, while it invites the majority to tyrannize over the minority, and gives the minority no redress, is not safe even for that majority itself. It is a system unbalanced, unchecked, without any definite rules to prevent it from running into abuse, and becoming a victim to its own excesses. The separation and complete independence of the several departments of the government is usually supposed to afford a sufficient security against an undue enlargement of the powers of any one of them. This is said to be the only real discovery in politics, which can be claimed by modern times; and it is generally considered a very *great* discovery, and, perhaps, the only contrivance by which public liberty can be preserved. The idea is wholly illusory. It is true, that public liberty could scarcely exist without such separation, and, for that reason, it was wisely adopted in our systems. But we should not rely on it, with too implicit a confidence, as affording in itself, any adequate barrier against the encroachments of power, or any adequate security for the rights and liberties of the people. I have little faith in these *balances* of government; because there is neither knowledge nor wisdom enough in man to render them accurate and permanent. In spite of every precaution against it, some one department will acquire an undue preponderance over the rest. The first excesses are apt to be committed by the legislature; and, in a consolidated government, such as the author supposes ours to be, there is a peculiar proneness to this. In all free governments, the democratic principle is continually extending itself. The people being possessed of all power, and feeling that they are subject to no authority except their own, learn, in the end, to consider the very restraints which they have voluntarily imposed upon themselves, in their constitution of government, as the mere creatures of their own will, which their own will may at any time destroy. Hence the legislature, the immediate representatives of the popular will, naturally assume upon themselves every power which is necessary to carry that will into effect. *This is not liberty*. True political liberty demands many and severe restraints; it requires protection against itself, and is no longer safe, when it refuses to submit to its own self-imposed discipline. But whatever power the legislature may assume, they seldom retain it long. They win it, not for themselves, but for the executive. All experience proves that this is a usual result, in every form of free government. In every age of the world, the few have found means to steal power from the many. But in *our* government, if it be indeed a consolidated one, such a result is absolutely inevitable. The powers which are expressly lodged in the executive, and the still greater powers which are assumed, because the Constitution does not expressly deny them, a patronage which has no limit, and acknowledges no responsibility, all these are quite enough to bring the legislature to the feet of the executive. Every new power, therefore, which is assumed by the *federal government*, does but add so much to the powers of the President. One by one, the powers of the other departments are swept away, or are wielded only at the will of the executive. This is not speculation; it is history; and those who have been so eager to increase the powers, and to diminish the responsibilities, of the federal government, may know, from their own experience, that they have labored only to aggrandize the executive department, and raise the President above the people. That officer is not, by the Constitution, and never was designed to be, anything more than a simple executive of the laws; but the principle which consolidates all power in the federal government clothes him with royal authority, and subjects every right and every interest of the people to his will. The boasted *balance*, which is supposed to be found in the separation and independence of the departments, is proved, even by our own experience, apart from all reasoning, to afford no sufficient security against this accumulation of powers. It is to be feared that the reliance which we place on it may serve to quiet our apprehensions, and render us less vigilant, than we ought to be, of the progress, sly, yet sure, which a vicious and cunning President may make towards absolute power.

And let us not sleep in the delusion that we shall derive all needful security from our own "intelligence and virtue." The people may, indeed, preserve their liberties forever, if they will take care to be always virtuous, always wise, and always vigilant. And they will be equally secure, if they can assure themselves that the rulers they may select will never abuse their trust, but will always understand and always pursue the true interests of the people. But, unhappily, there are no such people, and no such rulers. A government must be imperfect, indeed, if it require such a degree of virtue in the people as renders all government unnecessary. Government is founded, not in the virtues, but in the vices of mankind; not in their knowledge and wisdom, but in their ignorance and folly. Its object is to protect the weak, to restrain the violent, to punish the vicious, and to compel all to the performance of the duty which man owes to man in a social state. It is not a self-acting machine, which will go on and perform its work without human agency; it cannot be separated from the human beings who fill its places, set it in motion, and regulate and direct its operations. So long as these are liable to err in judgment, or to fail in virtue, so long will government be liable to run into abuses. Until all men shall become so perfect as not to require to be ruled, all governments professing to be free will require to be watched, guarded, checked and controlled. To do this effectually requires more than we generally find of public virtue and public intelligence. A great majority of mankind are much more sensible to their interests than to their rights. Whenever the people can be persuaded that it is their greatest interest to maintain their rights, then, and then only, will free government be safe from abuses.

Looking to our own federal government, apart from the States, and regarding it, as our author would have us, as a consolidated government of all the people of the United States, we shall not find in it this salutary countervailing interest. In an enlarged sense, it is, indeed, the greatest interest of all to support that government in its purity; for, although it is undoubtedly defective in many important respects, it is much the best that has yet been devised. Unhappily, however, the greatest interest of the whole is not *felt to be*, although in truth it is, the greatest interest of all the parts. This results from the fact, that our character is not homogeneous, and our pursuits are wholly different. Rightly understood, this fact should tend to bind us the more closely together, by showing us our dependence upon each other; and it should teach us the necessity of watching, with the greater jealousy, every departure from the strict principles of our union. It is a truth, however, no less melancholy than incontestable, that if this ever was the view of the people, it has ceased to be so. And it could not be otherwise. Whatever be the *theory* of our Constitution, its *practice*, of late years, has made it a consolidated government; the government of an irresponsible majority. If that majority can find, either in the pursuits of their own peculiar industry, or in the offices and emoluments which flow from the patronage of the government, an interest distinct from that of the minority, they will pursue that interest, and nothing will be left to the minority but the poor privilege of complaining. Thus the government becomes tyrannous and oppressive, precisely in proportion as its democratic principle is extended; and instead of the enlarged and general interest which should check and restrain it, a peculiar interest is enlisted, to extend its powers and sustain its abuses. Public virtue and intelligence avail little, in such a condition of things as this. That virtue falls before the temptations of interest which you present to it, and that intelligence, thus deprived of its encouraging hopes, serves only to point out new objects of unlawful pursuit, and suggest new and baser methods of attaining them.

This result could scarcely be brought about, if the federal government were allowed to rest on the principles upon which I have endeavored to place it. The checking and controlling influences which afford safety to public liberty, are not to be found in the government itself. The people cannot always protect themselves against their rulers; if they could, no free government, in past times, would have been overthrown. Power and patronage cannot easily be so limited and defined, as to rob them of their corrupting influences over the public mind. It is truly and wisely remarked by the Federalist, that "a power over a man's subsistence is a power over his will." As little as possible of this power should be entrusted to the federal government, and even that little should be watched by a power authorized and competent to arrest its abuses. That power can be found only in the States. In this consists the great superiority of the federative system over every other. In that system, the federal government is responsible, not directly to the people *en masse*, but to the people in their character of distinct political corporations. However easy it may be to steal power from *the people*, *governments* do not so readily yield it to one another. The confederated States confer on their common government only such power as they themselves cannot separately exercise, or such as can be better exercised by that government. They have, therefore, an equal interest, to give it power enough, and to prevent it from assuming too much. In their hands the power of interposition is attended with no danger; it may be safely lodged where there is no interest to abuse it.

Under a federative system, the people are not liable to be acted on, (at least, not to the same extent), by those influences which are so apt to betray and enslave them, under a consolidated government. Popular masses, acting under the excitements of the moment, are easily led into fatal errors. History is full of examples of the good and great sacrificed to the hasty judgments of infuriated multitudes, and of the most fatal public measures adopted under the excitements of the moment. How easy is it for the adroit and cunning to avail themselves of such occasions, and how impossible is it, for a people so acted on, to watch their rulers wisely, and guard themselves against the encroachments of power? In a federative system, this danger is avoided, so far as their common government is concerned. The right of interposition belongs, not to the people in the aggregate, but to the people in separate and comparatively small subdivisions. And even in these subdivisions, they can act only through the forms of their own separate governments. These are necessarily slow and deliberate, affording time for excitement to subside, and for passion to cool. Having to pass through their own governments, before they can reach that of the United States, they are forbidden to act, until they have had time for reflection, and for the exercise of a cool and temperate judgment. Besides, they are taught to look, not to one government only, for the protection and security of their rights, and not to feel that they owe obedience only to that. Conscious that they can find, in their own State governments, protection against the wrongs of the federal government, their feeling of dependence is less oppressive, and their judgments more free. And while their efforts to throw off oppression are not repressed by a feeling that there is no power to which they can appeal, these efforts are kept under due restraints, by a consciousness that they cannot be unwisely exerted, except to the injury of the people themselves. It is difficult to perceive how a federal government, established on correct principles, can ever be overthrown, except by external violence, so long as the federative principle is duly respected and maintained. All the requisite checks and balances will be found, in the right of the States to keep their common government within its proper sphere; and a sufficient security for the due exercise of that right is afforded by the fact, that it is the *interest* of the States to exercise it discreetly. So far as our own government is concerned, I venture to predict that it will become absolute and irresponsible, precisely in proportion as the rights of the States shall cease to be respected, and their authority to interpose for the correction of federal abuses shall be denied and overthrown.

It should be the object of every patriot in the United States to encourage a high respect for the State governments. The people should be taught to regard them as their greatest interest, and as the first objects of their duty and affection. Maintained in their just rights and powers, they form the true balance-wheel, the only effectual check upon federal encroachments. And it possesses as a check these distinguishing advantages over every other, that it can never be applied without great deliberation and caution, that it is certain in its effects, and that it is but little liable to abuse. It is true that a State *may* use its power for improper purposes, or on improper occasions; but the federal government is, to say the least of it, equally liable to dangerous errors and violations of trust. Shall we then leave that government free from all restraint, merely because the proper countervailing power is liable to abuse? Upon the same principle, we should abandon all the guards and securities, which we have so carefully provided in the Federal Constitution itself. The truth is, all checks upon government are more or less imperfect; for if it were not so, government itself would be perfect. But this is no reason why we should abandon it to its own will. We have only to apply to this subject our best discretion and caution, to confer no more power than is absolutely necessary, and to guard that power as carefully as we can. Perfection is not to be hoped for; but an approximation to it, sufficiently near to afford a reasonable security to our rights and liberties, is not unattainable. In the formation of the federal government we have been careful to limit its powers, and define its duties. Our object was to render it such that the people should feel an interest in sustaining it in its purity, for otherwise it could not long subsist. Upon the same principle, we should enlist the same interest in the wise and proper application of those checks, which its unavoidable imperfections render necessary. That interest is found in the States. Having created the federal government at their own free will, and for their own uses, why should they seek to destroy it? Having clothed it with a certain portion of their own powers, for their own benefit alone, why should they desire to render those powers inoperative and nugatory? The danger is, not that the States will interpose too often, but that they will rather submit to federal usurpations, than incur the risk of embarrassing that government, by any attempts to check and control it. Flagrant abuses alone, and such as public liberty cannot endure, will ever call into action this salutary and conservative power of the States.

But whether this check be the best or the worst in its nature, it is at least one which our system allows. It is not found *within* the Constitution but exists independent of it. As that Constitution was formed by sovereign States, they alone are authorized, whenever the question arises between them and their common government, to determine, in the last resort, what powers they intended to confer on it. This is an inseparable incident of sovereignty; a right which belongs to the States, simply because they have never surrendered it to any other power. But to render this right available for any good purpose, it is indispensably necessary to maintain the States in their proper position. If their people suffer them to sink into the insignificance of mere municipal corporations, it will be vain to invoke their protection against the gigantic power of the federal government. This is the point to which the vigilance of the people should be chiefly directed. Their highest interest is at home; their palladium is their own State governments. They ought to know that they can look nowhere else with perfect assurance of safety and protection. Let them then maintain those governments, not only in their rights, but in their dignity and influence. Make it the interest of their people to serve them; an interest strong enough to resist all the temptations of federal office and patronage. Then alone will their voice be heard with respect at Washington; then alone will their interposition avail to protect their own people against the usurpations of the great central power. It is vain to hope that the federative principle of our government can be preserved, or that anything can prevent it from running into the absolutism of consolidation, if we suffer the rights of the States to be filched way, and their dignity and influence to be lost, through our carelessness or neglect.

"The Union"

From *Construction Construed and Constitutions Vindicated*

By John Taylor of Caroline

1820

"The Union" from *Constructions Construed* and *Constitutions Vindicated*
by John Taylor of Caroline (1820)

The Union

Who made it? "We, the people of the United States." But who were they? The associated inhabitants of each state, or the unassociated inhabitants of all the states. This question is an exposition, either of the ignorance or the design of construction. If there is no difficulty in answering it, construction ought to be laughed at for playing the fool; but if it gives the wrong answer, as supposing it to furnish contrary inferences to the right one, it ought to be suspected of playing the knave. At least an attempt to construe away a fact, known to everybody, is a very fine specimen of its character when aiming at an accession of power. It has been imagined, that by considering the union as the act of the people, in their natural, and not in their political associated capacity, some aspect of consolidation might be shed over the country, and that the federal government might thereby acquire more power. But I cannot discern that the construction of the constitution will be affected in the smallest degree, by deducing it from either source, provided a sound authority is allowed to the source selected. Every stipulation, sentence, word and letter; and every donation, reservation, division and restriction, will be exactly the same, whichever is preferred. A man, having two titles, may distinguish himself by which he pleases, in making a contract; and whichever he uses, he remains himself. So the people having two titles or capacities, one arising from an existing association, the other from the natural right of self-government, may enter into a compact under either, but are themselves still; and their acts are equally obligatory, whichever they may select. Politicians may therefore indulge their taste in deducing the constitution of the union from either, but whichever they may fancy, no sound ground will thence result for their differing in the construction of it.

Nevertheless, to take away the pretext, however unsubstantial, for a different construction of the constitution, on account of the capacity or title under which the people acted in its establishment, it is material to ascertain the meaning of the phrase "we the people of the United States"; towards which, let us run over most of the state constitutions.

New Hampshire. "The people of this state have *the sole and exclusive right* of governing themselves as a free, *sovereign* and independent *state.* Every subject of this *state.* In the government of this *state.* The people inhabiting the territory formerly called the province of New Hampshire, do hereby solemnly and *mutually agree with each other* to form themselves into a free, *sovereign* and independent *body politick or state.* That the *state may be equally represented.* I do swear that I will bear faith and true *allegiance to the state* of New Hampshire."

Massachusetts. "The body politick is formed by voluntary *association of individuals.* The people of this commonwealth have the sole right of governing themselves as a free, *sovereign* and independent *state.* The people do hereby *mutually agree with each other,* to form themselves into a free, *sovereign* and independent body politick *or state.*"

New York. "This convention, in the name and by the authority of the good *people of this state.* The legislature of this *state.* No members of this *state* shall be disfranchised. Delegates to represent this *state* in the general congress of the *United States.* Be it enacted by the people of the *state.*"

Pennsylvania. "*We the people* of the commonwealth of Pennsylvania ordain. The legislature of a free *state.* All government originates from the people and is founded in compact only."

Delaware. "The people of this *state.* The government shall be called the Delaware *state.* The legislature of this *state.* The general assembly of this state. There shall be no establishment of any one religious sect in this *state.*"

Maryland. "The *people of this state* ought to have the sole and exclusive right of regulating the *internal government* thereof. The *legislature of this state.* The delegates to congress from this *state* shall be chosen by joint ballot of both houses of assembly. I will be

"The Union" from *Constructions Construed* and *Constitutions Vindicated*
by John Taylor of Caroline (1820)

faithful and bear true allegiance to the *state*."

Virginia. "All power is derived from the people. Magistrates are their trustees or servants. A well-regulated militia is the proper defense of a *free state*."

North Carolina. "The *people of this state* have the sole and exclusive right of regulating the *internal government* thereof. Monopolies are contrary to the genius of a free *state*. All commissions shall run in the name of the *state* of North Carolina. The legislature of this *state*. The constitution of this *state*."

South Carolina. "The legislative authority of this *state*. The several election districts in this *state* shall elect. The style of process shall be 'The *state* of South Carolina, and conclude against the peace and dignity of the *state*.' I swear to preserve the constitution of this *state* and of the *United States*."

Georgia. "Members of the legislature shall swear to promote the good of the *state*, to bear true allegiance to the same, and to observe the constitution. To make laws necessary for the good of the *state*. Citizens and inhabitants of this *state*."

Vermont. "The people are the sole source of power. They have the exclusive right of *internal government*. All officers of government are their servants. Legislative and executive business of this *state*. The people have a right to exact from their legislators and magistrates the good government of the *state*. The legislature of a free and *sovereign state*. Shall be entitled to all the privileges of a freeman of this *state*. Every officer shall swear to be faithful to the *state* of Vermont, and to do nothing injurious to the constitution or *government* thereof."

Without further quotations, let us demonstrate the force of these, extracted from a majority of the state constitutions, to fix the meaning of the term "state" according to the public judgment, by substituting the word "government" for it. They would then read as follows:

"The people of this *government* have the sole and exclusive right of governing themselves as a free, *sovereign* and independent *government*."

"In the government of this *government*."

"That the *government* may be equally represented."

"The people of this *government* ought to have the sole and exclusive right of regulating the *internal government thereof*."

"The legislature of this *government*."

"I will be faithful and bear true allegiance to the *government*."

"The several election districts in this *government* shall elect."

"Members of the legislature shall swear to promote the good of the *government* and to make laws for the good of the *government*."

"Citizens and inhabitants of this *government*."

"The people have a right to exact from their legislators and magistrates the good government of the *government*."

"Commissions shall be in the name of the freemen of the *government*."

It would be an incivility to the reader, to subjoin to these quotations, many arguments, to prove, that the term "state" is not in any one instance used in reference to all the people of the United States, either as composing a single state, or as being about to compose a single state. Used geographically, it refers to state territory; used politically, it refers to the inhabitants of this territory, united by mutual consent into a civil society. The sovereignty of this association, the allegiance due to it, and its right to internal government, are all positively asserted. The terms "state and government" far from being synonymous, are used to convey different ideas; and the latter is never recognized as possessing any species of sovereignty.

It next behooves us to consider whether the term "states" has changed

"The Union" from *Constructions Construed* and *Constitutions Vindicated*
by John Taylor of Caroline (1820)

its meaning, by being transplanted from its original nursery, into the constitution of the United States; and is there used to designate all the inhabitants of the United States, as constituting one great state; or whether it is recognized in the same sense in which it had been previously used by most or all of the state constitutions.

The plural "states" rejects the idea, that the people of all the states considered themselves as one state. The word "united" is an averment of pre-existing social compacts, called states; and these consisted of the people of each separate state. It admits the existence of political societies able to contract with each other, and who had previously contracted. And the words "more perfect union" far from implying that the old parties to the old union were superseded by new parties, evidently mean, that these same old parties were about to amend their old union.

But the parties, though recognized as being the same, were not strictly so. The authority of the people of each state is resorted to in the last union, in preference to that of the government of each state, by which the old confederation was formed. This circumstance by no means weakens the force of the last observation, because the recognition of existing political parties able to contract, remains the same. The states, in referring to the old union, only admit themselves to have been bound by their governments, as they possessed the right of making treaties. But as the state governments were the parties to the first confederation, and as such, had a mutual right to destroy that treaty, this danger suggests another reason for the style and principles of the new union. Among its improvements, that by which it is chiefly made "more perfect," was the substitution of the authority of "the people of the United States" for that of the governments of the United States; not with an intention of excluding from the new union the idea of a compact between the states, but of placing that compact upon better ground, than that upon which it previously rested.

The term "union" has never been applied to describe a government, established by the consent of individuals; nor do any of our state constitutions use it in that sense. They speak indeed of individuals "uniting" to form a government, not to form a union; and I do not recollect that a single compact between individuals for the establishment of a government, has ever been called a union; though a multitude of cases exist, in which that name has been given to agreements between independent states. If therefore this term comprised the whole evidence, to prove that our union was the act of distinct bodies politick, composed of the people within different geographical boundaries, and not of a number of people, encircled by one line, without any such discrimination, it would be sufficient.

But the constitution itself furnishes the plainest correspondent evidence, in its origin, establishment and terms. The members of the convention which formed it, were chosen by states, and voted by states, without any regard to the number of people in each state. It was adopted by thirteen votes, without respecting the same principle. Now what was represented by these voters; the territory of each state, or the people of each state? The terms "United States" must refer to one or the other. If to the former, then the territories of each state entered into a compact "to form a more perfect union, establish justice, ensure domestic tranquility, provide for the common defense, promote the general welfare, and secure the blessings of liberty to *ourselves* and our *posterity*." *The posterity of territories.* If to the latter, it was the people of each state, who by compact in their political capacity, by giving one vote each, formed the union.

The concords with this opinion present themselves at every step, throughout the compact.

The house of representatives are to be chosen by the people of the *several states*, not by the people comprised within the territories of all. The right of choice is confined to the electors of the most numerous branch of the *state legislatures*. Thus the right of suffrage is placed upon different grounds in different states. Had the constitution of the United States been the act of all the people inhabiting the territory of the United States, this right would have been made uniform; but being the act of the people of each state, in their existing political capacity, the right of suffrage of course remained as it had been settled by each in forming its society.

Each state may elect these representatives by a general ticket, as some have done; and however they may have districted themselves by their own act for their own reasons, the recognizance of state individuality by the constitution is as strong, as if they had not done so. The modes of choosing both the president and senate, coincide also with the opinion, that the constitution considered the union as the act of bodies politick called states; and not as the act of a consolidated nature; and it seems to have settled its own construction, by providing in the case of no election of a president by electors, that he shall be chosen by the house of representatives, "the votes to be taken by states, the representation from *each state having one vote.*"

As the great political departments of the federal government, legislative and executive, emanated from the societies called states, so they are made dependent upon them, in the mode prescribed for amending the constitution of the union; because the authors had the right of altering their own work. Had this constitution originated from, or been made by the people inhabiting the territories of the whole union, its amendment would have remained to them, as the amendment of the state constitutions belongs to the people of a state. But as such a body of associated people, did not exist, the amendment of the union is left in the hands of the existing bodies politick, to which, as its authors, it obviously belonged. No majority in congress can either call a convention, or amend the constitution; but the legislatures of two-thirds of the states may compel congress to call one, and those of three-fourths, may amend it. Thus, a supremacy of the states, not only over congress, but over the whole constitution, is twice acknowledged; first, by their power over the legislative and executive departments instituted for executing the union; and secondly, by their power over the union itself. I cannot conceive that the constitution could have contained anything more hostile to the doctrine "that the sovereignty or supremacy over the government of the union, rested in the people of the United States, not in their political, but natural capacity." It clearly discloses an opinion, that there were no such people, politically speaking; nor can I discern a vestige of the people inhabiting the territories of the United States, having ever formed themselves, or attempted to form themselves, into any political society or civil government. By this new doctrine, however, the checks provided to control the powers of the government of the union are ingeniously evaded. It asserts, that the government of the union is responsible to the sovereignty of the people residing throughout the union, and not to the sovereignty of the people residing in each state. Now as an effective sovereignty of the people can only result from their having constituted themselves into a civil society, and the first people having never done so, an acknowledgment of a sovereignty which does not exist, only annuls that which does; and escapes altogether from any species of loyalty to this superior authority. It brings us back to the old ground of a tacit compact between governments and subjects. The people of each state invested their governments with limited powers. They have also established a government of the union with powers infinitely more limited, than those originally bestowed on the state governments. But if a tacit social compact between this last government, and the people individually of all the states, should be admitted, all these specifications would be abolished; because, as it is unwritten, the government of the union might construe it as was most convenient to itself, as all governments have done, which have condescended to acknowledge implied obligations only. The only difference between the Europeans and ourselves would be, that though some of their governments hardly allow of this silent social compact, none acknowledge the sovereignty of the people; whereas here this sovereignty would be denied, where it operatively exists, and acknowledged, where it does not exist at all; so that we should still possess over the government of the union, all the advantages generally reaped from "we are, gentlemen, your most obedient servants," whilst the story of Saturn would be gradually reversed.

The eleventh amendment prohibits a *construction* by which the rights retained by the people shall *be denied or disparaged*; and

"The Union" from *Constructions Construed* and *Constitutions Vindicated*
by John Taylor of Caroline (1820)

the twelfth "reserves *to the states respectively or to the people* the powers not delegated to t*he United States*, nor prohibited *to the states*." The precision of these expressions is happily contrived to defeat a construction, by which the origin of the union, or the sovereignty of the states, could be rendered at all doubtful. "Powers are reserved to the people." "The people," says Johnson, are "those who compose a community." In a political instrument, the term exclusively possesses a collective, inclusive, and social sense, and is never used to describe a number of men in a state of nature. A people is a collective being. No people or community has ever been composed in the United States, except by the inhabitants of each state, associating distinctly from every other state, by their own separate consent. Thus, a people in each state was constituted, and these separate communities confederated, first by the instrumentality of their separate governments, and secondly by the separate authority of the people composing each state. Common consent is necessary to constitute a people, and no such consent, expressly or impliedly, can be shown, by which all the inhabitants of the United States have ever constituted themselves into one people. This could not have been effected without destroying every people constituted within each state, as one political being called a people cannot exist within another.

The rights of a people are indivisible; and if a great people be compounded of several smaller nations, as it inherently possesses the right of self-government, it must absorb the same right of self-government in its component parts; just as the rights of individuals are absorbed by the communities into which they constitute themselves. Therefore, had a people been constituted, by melting down the little nations into one great nation, those little nations must have lost the right of self-government, because they would no longer have been a people. As it was never imagined, that the individuals inhabiting all the states had constituted themselves into one people, so there has never appeared from this imaginary body politick, the least attempt towards claiming or exercising the right of self-government; nor is the government of the union subjected to its control or modification. Not a single one of the United States would have consented to have dissolved its people, to have reunited them into one great people, and to have received state governments or unrestricted legislation from this great people, so ignorant of local circumstances, and so different in local habits. This reasoning would I think have been sufficient to ascertain the people by whom the constitution was made, had it contained no internal evidence of the sense in which it uses that term. But if the phrase "we the people of the United States" refers to the people of each state, the argument is superfluous, and the decision of the constitution itself, decisive.

The powers reserved are those "not delegated by the constitution." They could only be *reserved* by those who possessed them. They were not powers possessed by a consolidated people of all the states, but by a distinct people of each state; and as those who reserved were those who delegated, it follows, either that the reservation was to a consolidated people of all the states, or that the delegation of powers flowed from the people of the separate states. Perhaps the interpolation of a grantor and reserver of powers into the constitution, who had nothing either to grant or to reserve, may have arisen from an erroneous construction of the word "or." If the remark just made is correct, consistency decides its true meaning. "Are reserved to the states respectively *or* to the people." This word is used either to couple synonyms, or to denote opposition. The words "states and people" had the same, and also a different meaning: The same, as an associated people constituted a state; and a different meaning, from the right of self-government attached to mankind. But another construction seems to me to be the true one. "Or" is used merely to conjoin two words considered as completely synonymous; and the latter is introduced as an expletive of the former, lest it should be interpreted to mean "governments." The word "states" had been so often used in the constitution, that it was necessary to fix its meaning; and this amendment was intended to remove the suspicion of a tendency in the constitution towards consolidation, with which it had been charged previously to its adoption; by defining "states and people" as words synonymously used, effectually to defeat the

"The Union" from *Constructions Construed* and *Constitutions Vindicated*
by John Taylor of Caroline (1820)

pretense, that the term "people" meant the people of all the states, instead of the people, "*respectively*" of each state. A construction which supposes that all the inhabitants of all the states, and not the people of each state, were meant, would produce consequences which never could have been contemplated. The reservation would have been in favor of two incongruous objects, and therefore both could not reap its benefits. Being in the disjunctive, it might have been fulfilled by acknowledging the right of either, although the other should get nothing. By selecting the inhabitants of all the states in one mass, as the assignee of the reserved powers, the government of the union might extend their own powers; since there could be no loss, in conceding powers to those who could neither receive, exercise, nor preserve them.

In one other view, highly gratifying, these two amendments correspond with the construction I contend for. Several previous amendments had stipulated for personal or individual rights, as the government of the union was invested with a limited power of acting upon persons; these stipulate for political conventional rights. But different modes are pursued. By the first, certain specified aggressions are forbidden; by the second, all the rights and powers not delegated are reserved. The first mode is imperfect, as the specified aggressions may be avoided, and yet oppression might be practiced in other forms. By the second, specification is transferred to the government of the union; and the states, instead of being the grantees of limited rights, which might have been an acknowledgment of subordination, are the grantors of limited powers; and retain a supremacy which might otherwise have been tacitly conceded, as has been often done by the acceptance of franchises from monarchs or other sovereigns. Thus, the powers reserved are only exposed to specified deductions, whilst those delegated are limited, with an injunction that the enumeration of certain rights shall not be construed to disparage those retained though not specified, by not having been parted with. The states, instead of receiving, bestowed powers; and in confirmation of their authority, reserved every right they had not conceded, whether it is particularly enumerated, or tacitly retained. Among the former, are certain modes by which they can amend the constitution; among the latter, is the original right by which they created it.

When we have discovered who made a treaty, we have also discovered where the right of construction resides. Mr. Jefferson, Mr. Pinckney, Mr. Marshall, and Mr. Gerry, in their negotiations with revolutionary France, have furnished us with an admirable treatise, both to fix the residence of the right, and to display the wantonness of construction, assumed without right. Presidents Washington and Adams, all the successive members of the cabinet and congress itself, concurred in the principles advanced by these gentlemen. They prove, that an exclusive right of construction in one party, is a degradation of the other to a state of inferiority and dependence. Their arguments might be applied with great force in many views to our subject. If the states made the union, they demonstrate, that the same consent, necessary to create, is necessary to construe. Wherever the creating consent resided, there we are directed to look for the construing consent. It would be a much grosser violation of their principles, for no party to a treaty to usurp an exclusive right of construing it, than for one party to do so. As neither the executive, legislative nor judicial departments of the state or federal governments have ever consented to the union, no one of these departments can have an exclusive right of construing it. But if they did consent, and by that consent are parties, still the right is mutual. And if they are all to be considered as the co-ordinate departments or creatures of "the people of the United States," they derive a mutual right of construction, from the mutual right possessed by the states which they represent. Suppose our legislative and judicial departments had fixed their own rights by a treaty between themselves, in the words of the general or state constitutions; would not each have possessed an unsubservient right of construction? If this right would be mutual in the case supposed, what hinders it from being also mutual, if these departments are created by an authority superior to both, and invested with distinct and limited agencies. Each trustee is subject to the supervision of his employer, and neither liable to a usurpation of another, any more than several co-ordinate ambassadors, would be to a claim of one to prescribe the duties of the rest, and regulate their consciences. It is easiest for an exclusive power of construction, where the limits of respective territories are hardest to define, to make conquests which will destroy balances, and break down restrictions; and therefore its interdiction in such cases is more necessary, than in others.

I conclude this section with a quotation from the Federalist. "The assent and ratification of the people, not as individuals composing one entire nation, but as composing the distinct and independent states to which they belong, are the sources of the constitution. It is therefore not a national, but a federal compact."

New American

THAT FREEDOM SHALL NOT PERISH

STAY INFORMED.

STAY FREE.

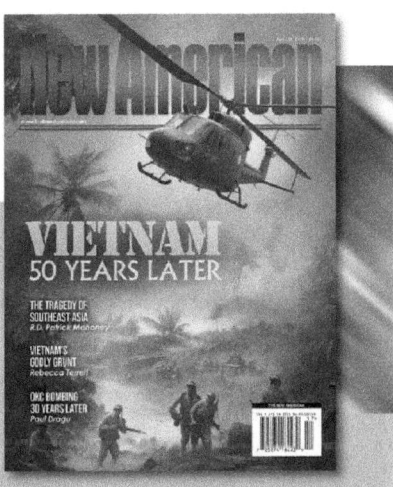

Are you looking for reliable news that cuts through the noise and delivers the truth about current events, government overreach, and the erosion of our liberties? *The New American* magazine is your go-to source for insightful analysis, principled reporting, and unapologetic advocacy for the Constitution.

For decades, we've kept readers informed about the issues that matter most — tyranny, globalism, and the ongoing fight for freedom. Don't settle for the mainstream narrative. Equip yourself with knowledge and stand on the side of liberty.

Scan the QR code to subscribe and join a growing community of informed patriots!

www.TheNewAmerican.com

The fight for liberty needs YOU. The John Birch Society has been at the forefront of defending the Constitution and opposing the encroachment of tyranny for over six decades. Now more than ever, patriots like you are essential in the battle to preserve our nation's founding principles.

Join us in our mission to restore America through education, activism, and unwavering dedication to the cause of liberty. Become part of a network of citizens committed to preserving the values that made our country great.

 Scan the QR code to join The John Birch Society and make your voice heard!

The Official Store of The John Birch Society

To order extra copies of this book, go to ShopJBS.org or call 1-800-342-6491

How Can I Make a Difference?

GETTING STARTED IS AS EASY AS 1,2,3

1. Sign up for JBS news and action alerts
- Stay informed with free content
- Visit www.JBS.org/e-newsletter to sign up now

2. Contact your elected representatives
- Local, state, and federal officials represent you
- Visit www.JBS.org/act-now for contact information

3. Join The John Birch Society
- National concerted action multiplies your impact
- Visit www.JBS.org/join to apply for membership today

The John Birch Society

P.O. Box 8040
Appleton, WI 54912-8040
(920) 749-3780 • **JBS.org**

"Less government, more responsibility,
and — with God's help — a better world."

www.ingramcontent.com/pod-product-compliance
Lightning Source LLC
LaVergne TN
LVHW050044090426
835510LV00043B/2867